Vinay

An Adventure

methuen | drama

LONDON · NEW YORK · OXFORD · NEW DELHI · SYDNEY

METHUEN DRAMA
Bloomsbury Publishing Plc
50 Bedford Square, London, WC1B 3DP, UK
1385 Broadway, New York, NY 10018, USA

BLOOMSBURY, METHUEN DRAMA and the Methuen Drama logo are
trademarks of Bloomsbury Publishing Plc

First published in Great Britain 2018

For legal purposes the Acknowledgements on p. 2
constitute an extension of this copyright page.

Cover design by StudioDoug

Photography by Bronwen Sharp

A catalogue record for this book is available from the British Library.

Library of Congress Cataloging-in-Publication Data

ISBN: PB: 978-1-3501-0286-6
ePDF: 978-1-3501-0287-3
eBook: 978-1-3501-0288-0

Series: Modern Plays

Typeset by Mark Heslington Ltd, Scarborough, North Yorkshire
Printed and bound in Great Britain

Bush Theatre

AN ADVENTURE

by Vinay Patel

6 September – 20 October 2018
Bush Theatre, London

CAST

Older Jyoti	Nila Aalia
David	Martins Imhangbe
Joy/Sonal	Aysha Kala
Older Rasik	Selva Rasalingam
Rasik	Shubham Saraf
Jyoti	Anjana Vasan

CREATIVE TEAM

Playwright	Vinay Patel
Director	Madani Younis
Associate Director	Deborah Pugh
Designer	Rosanna Vize
Design Associate	Anna Lewis
Lighting Designer	Sally Ferguson
Sound Designer	Ed Clarke
Costume Supervisor	Lily O'Hara
Video Designer	Louise Rhodes-Brown
Dramaturg	Deirdre O'Halloran
Production Manager	Michael Ager
Company Stage Manager	Eleanor Dear
Assistant Stage Manager	Ana Carter
Technical Stage Manager	Caoimhe Young

CAST

Nila Aalia Older Jyoti

Nila has most recently been filming *A Discovery Of Witches - All Souls Trilogy* (Bad Wolf Ltd) as well as Jaume Collet-Serra's action-thriller *The Commuter*.

Nila's previous theatre work includes: *Bombay Dreams* (RUG), *Elder Latimer is In Love* (Arcola Theatre), *Instant Celebrity* (Silver Star Productions), *Ramayana* (Sita Theatre), *Mahabharata* (Gita Productions), *Vagina Monologues* (I.W.D), *Frau Aus Ton, Ogboimba, Zweite Wirklichkeit* (PAZ Munich), *Schwanensee Müllkippe* (B.W. Gung, Ulm), *Waiting for Godot, Antigone* (Eldred Theatre,Cl.USA). Other film credits include: *A Good Year* (Stripe Productions), *Diverted* (Big Tree Productions), *No Place Like Home* (Mary Nighy). Television includes: *Wolfblood* (CBBC), *The Rebel* (Retort), *The Intern* (Boundless), *Scott & Bailey* (ITV), *Silent Witness* (BCC), *Whitechapel* (Carnival Films), *Hollyoaks* (Lime Pictures), *Outnumbered* (Hat Trick), *Bike Squad* (Hat Trick), *5 Days* (BBC/HBO), *A Touch Of Frost* (ITV), *Torchwood* (BBC), *Casualty* (BBC), *Doctors* (BBC), *EastEnders* (BBC), *Life isn't all Ha Ha He He* (BBC/Hat Trick), *Taggart* (ITV1/SMG TV), *If Drugs Were Legal* (BBC), *Spooks* (BBC/Kudos).

Martins Imhangbe David

Martins has previously appeared in the Bush Theatre production of *The Royale*. Martins trained at Central School of Speech and Drama.

Previous theatre includes: *Absolute Hell* (National Theatre), *Barbershop Chronicles* (National Theatre), *Luce* (Southwark Playhouse), *Octagon* (Arcola Theatre), *The Skriker* (The Royal Exchange Theatre), *Lionboy* (Complicite), *Das Ding* (New Diorama), *Romeo and Juliet* (Orange Tree Theatre), *Cinderella: A Fairytale* (Unicorn Theatre), *A Human Being Died That Night* (Hampstead Theatre), *Sold* (Edinburgh Fringe, winner of Amnesty Freedom of Expression Award) and *What Does it Take* (National Theatre).

Aysha Kala Joy/Sonal

Aysha trained at the Royal Welsh College of Music and Drama and was named a BAFTA Breakthrough Brit of 2015.

Her previous theatre includes: *Obsession* (Barbican), *Frogman* (Shoreditch Town Hall), *Punk Play, Farragut North* (Southwark Playhouse), *Djinns of Eidgah* (Royal Court), *Khadija is 18* (Finborough Theatre) and *Much Ado About Nothing* (RSC). Aysha has also appeared in *Indian Summers, Vicious* and *Shameless* (Channel 4). Her film work includes: *Second Coming* and *Jadoo*.

Selva Rasalingam Older Rasik

Selva's previous theatre includes: *The Captive Queen* (Sam Wanamaker, Shakespeare's Globe), *Disgraced* (English Theatre Frankfurt), *The Riots* (Tricycle), *Guantanamo: Honor Bound to Defend Freedom* (Tricycle, New Ambassadors), *Midnight's Children* (RSC), *On the Record* (Arcola), *The Nightmares of Carlos Fuentes* (Arcola). Television includes: *Versailles, EastEnders, Silent Witness, The Missing, Hustle, Casualty, Luther, Doctor Who, Spooks* (BBC), *Run* (Channel 4), *Strike Back, Legends, The Borgias* (Sky). Film credits include: *Damascus Cover, The Mummy, Gospels of Matthew, Mark, Luke and John, Prince of Persia, The Veteran, Risen*.

Shubham Saraf Rasik

Shubham trained at the Guildhall School of Music and Drama. Previous theatre includes: *Hamlet, As You Like It, Lions and Tigers* (Globe Theatre). Television includes: *The Bodyguard* (BBC) and *Fresh Meat* (Channel 4). Film includes: *Overlord, The Cut* and *Honour*.

Anjana Vasan Jyoti

Anjana trained at the Royal Welsh College of Music and Drama.

Previous theatre includes: *Summer and Smoke* (Almeida), *King Lear, A Midsummer Night's Dream* (Globe Theatre), *Life of Galileo* (Young Vic), *Image of an Unknown Young Woman* (Gate Theatre), *Dara; Behind The Beautiful Forevers* (National Theatre), *Macbeth* (Park Armory New York/Manchester International Festival), *The Taming of the Shrew, Much Ado About Nothing* (RSC), *The Radicalisation of Bradley Manning* (National Theatre Wales). Television includes: *Brexit, Pls Like, Hang Ups, Ill Behaviour, Black Mirror, Call the Midwife, Fresh Meat*.

CREATIVE TEAM

Vinay Patel Playwright

Vinay's debut play, *True Brits*, opened at the Edinburgh Fringe 2014, transferred to the Bush Theatre and went on to headline the 2015 Vault Festival.

His television debut *Murdered By My Father* was commissioned for BBC3 and later repeated on BBC1. It won the Royal Television Society award for Best Single Drama before going on to be nominated for three BAFTAs and Vinay was named a BAFTA Breakthrough Brit for his work.

He has since written for Paines Plough, ITV, Channel 4 and the BFI, as well as contributing to the bestselling collection of essays, *The Good Immigrant*. Vinay is currently working on series 11 of *Doctor Who* and developing work for the BBC.

Madani Younis Director

Madani took over as Artistic Director of the Bush Theatre in 2012. He directed the critically acclaimed UK premiere of *The Royale* in 2015 which was revived in 2016. In 2013 he won the Groucho Club Maverick Award for the theatre, following the most successful season in the theatre's history, which played to 99% capacity. Also for the Bush Theatre he has directed *The Principles of Cartography* as part of *Black Lives, Black Words, Zaida and Aadam* as part of *This Place We Know, Perseverance Drive* and *Chalet Lines*.

Madani is currently working as a member of the Mayor of London's Cultural Board.

Prior to his appointment at the Bush Theatre, he was Artistic Director of Freedom Studios in Bradford, Yorkshire, where his work included the site-specific work, *The Mill – City of Dreams*. He has also worked nationally and internationally as a theatre director, writer and practitioner. He was previously Director of Red Ladder Theatre Company's Asian Theatre School where he directed *Silent Cry, Free World and Streets of Rope*.

He originally trained in film, and his debut short film *Ellabellapumpanella*, commissioned by the UK Film Council, was screened at the Cannes Film Festival in May 2007. He was the recipient of the Decibel Award at the South Bank Awards show in 2006.

Deborah Pugh Associate Director

Deb originally trained at École Internationale de Théâtre Jacques Lecoq and is a core member of Theatre Ad Infinitum, developing and performing original work with them since 2007.

Previous work as a movement director includes: *One Flew Over the Cuckoo's Nest* (Sheffield Crucible), *Stan* (Art with Heart), *A Short History of Tractors in Ukrainian* (Hull Truck Theatre), *The Twits* (Curve, Leicester and Rose Theatre, Kingston), *Bucket List* (Bristol Old Vic), *Light* (Barbican & London International Mime Festival), *Ballad of the Burning Star* (international tour), *Translunar Paradise* (Barbican & international tour), *Declaration* (Lowry Theatre), *Bassett* (Sheffield Crucible), *Kristin Lavransdatter* (North Wall) and *Breakin' Convention* (Sadler's Wells).

Rosanna Vize Designer

Rosanna trained at Bristol Old Vic Theatre School as a theatre designer. She has worked regularly as an assistant to Anna Fleischle and was the resident design assistant for the RSC from Sep 2014 – Sep 2015. She was a Linbury Prize Finalist in 2013 working with English Touring Opera and is currently one of the Jerwood Young Designers.

Theatre includes: *King Lear* (Globe Theatre), *The Earthworks & Myth* (RSC), *The Almighty Sometimes* (Royal Exchange Manchester), *Yous Two, The Phlebotomist* (Hampstead Theatre), *Henry I* (Reading Between the Lines), *Girls* (Soho Theatre, Hightide & Talawa Theatre), *FUP, Noye's Fludde* (Kneehigh Theatre), *Dark Land Lighthouse, St Joan of the Stockyards, A Thousand Seasons Passed, The Tinder Box, The Last Days of Mankind, Talon* (Bristol Old Vic), *Diary of a Madman, The Rise and Shine of Comrade Fiasco* (Gate Theatre), *Infinite Lives, Coastal Defenses* (Tobacco Factory Theatres), *Banksy: The Room in the Elephant* (Tobacco Factory Theatres and Traverse Theatre), *Edward Gants Amazing Feats of Loneliness, Wicked Lady* (Bristol Old Vic Theatre School), *The Picture of John Grey* (The Old Red Lion), *Measure for Measure* (Oxford School of Drama).

Opera includes: *Don Giovanni* (Hampstead Garden Opera), *A Midsummer Night's Dream* (RSC & Garsington Opera).

Anna Lewis Design Associate

Anna is a Jerwood Young Designer and her work is supported by an MGCfutures Bursary.

Recent theatre includes: *EAST* (Kings Head Theatre – Offie nominated for Best Production), *Deadly Dialogues* (Edinburgh), *Life According to Saki* (Edinburgh, Fourth Street Theatre New York – Winner of the Carol Tambor Best of Edinburgh Award), *A New Coat for Christmas, Snowflakes, Jane Eyre* and *Rosencrantz and Guildenstern are Dead* (Oxford Playhouse) and *After October* (Finborough Theatre – nominated for best costume at the Off West End Awards). Other selected work includes: *Three Writers Walk Into a Forest* (Theatre503), *Obamaology* (Finborough Theatre), *Two Roads* (Vault Festival), *Twelfth Night* (Southwark Playhouse, The Dell Stratford, Saitama Theatre, Tokyo Metropolitan Theatre, Yvonne Arnaud), *The Sorcerer* (Buxton Opera House), *Bound* (Pegasus Theatre) and *Ghosts* (Greenwich Theatre).

Anna was Lead Costume Supervisor on Turner Prize-winning *we're here because we're here* (National Theatre). She works regularly at the National Theatre in the costume and props departments, most recently as props buyer on *The Lehman Trilogy, Amadeus, Angels in America*, and *St George and the Dragon*, and was part of the V&A's inaugural Salisbury Gallery exhibition *Opera: Passion, Power and Politics*.

Sally Ferguson Lighting Designer

Sally's credits include: *Jess And Joe Forever* (Orange Tree), *The Two Boroughs Project* (Young Vic), *Sweet Charity* (Manchester Royal Exchange), *We Wait In Joyful Hope, And Then Come The Nightjars, Many Moons* (Theatre 503), *Shiver, Lost In Yonkers* (Watford Palace Theatre), *The Sleeping Beauties* (Sherman Cymru), *As You Like It, Floyd Collins* (Southwark Playhouse), *Hag, The Girl With The Iron Claws* (Wrong Crowd/Soho Theatre), *Microcosm* (Soho Theatre), *The Imagination Museum* (UK tour), *Slowly* (Riverside Studios), *Cosi Fan Tutte* (Village Underground), *The Devils Festival* (The Print

Room), *The Marriage Of Figaro* (Wilton's Music Hall), *The Wonder! A Woman Keeps A Secret* (BAC).

Ed Clarke Sound Designer

Ed has previously worked at the Bush Theatre on *The Royale*, *The Invisible*, *Perseverance Drive* and *Fear*. His other theatre credits include *All We Ever Wanted Was Everything* (Middle Child Theatre), *A Super Happy Story (About Feeling Super Sad)*, (Silent Uproar), *A Christmas Carol* and *A Short History Of Tractors In Ukrainian* (Hull Truck Theatre), *Showboat* (New London Theatre), *The Infidel* (Theatre Royal Stratford East), *Orpheus* (Little Bulb Theatre at BAC and worldwide), *Baddies* (Unicorn Theatre), *The Realness*, *Politrix*, *Phoenix*, *Knife Edge* and *Babylon* (The Big House), *Beauty and the Beast* (Young Vic and worldwide), Danny Boyle's *Frankenstein* (Olivier, National Theatre – Olivier Award nomination 2012), *Backbeat* (Duke of York's Theatre), *The Mysteries* and *The Good Hope* (National Theatre), *The Railway Children* (Waterloo International Station and Roundhouse Theatre Toronto), *Fatal Attraction* (Theatre Royal Haymarket), *Backbeat* (Duke of York's), *His Teeth* (Only Connect Theatre), *Baby Doll* (Albery Theatre), *Alex* (Arts Theatre, UK and international tour), *Old Times* and *A Doll's House* (Donmar Warehouse).

Lily O'Hara Costume Supervisor

Lily has been designing costumes for film and theatre for the last three years. She graduated from the University of Manchester in 2014 with an upper second class honours in History of Art.

Her television credits include: ITV, BBC and Channel 4, she has also designed the costumes for many short independent films and music videos. She has additional skills in costume supervision and construction, scenic art, prop making, set building and hair and make up. Her theatre credits include: The Other Palace, Bush Theatre, Punchdrunk, The Arcola, The Park Theatre, The Peacock, Black Heath Halls, Tricycle Theatre, Battersea Arts Centre, Finborough Theatre, Theatre 503, Waterloo East, Waterloo Vaults, Hackney Empire, Southwark Playhouse, Oxford Playhouse, Edinburgh Fringe festival, The Bridewell Theatre and Secret Cinema.

Louise Rhodes-Brown Video Designer

Louise is a highly skilled Video and Projection Designer specialising in video for theatre and live events. She trained in Motion Graphic Design at Ravenbourne College.

Recent theatre and live events include: *Br'er Cotton*, *The Swallowing Dark* (Theatre 503), *Rothschild & Sons*, *The Ugly One*, *The Trial of Jane Fonda* (Park Theatre), *Inside Pussy Riot* (The Saatchi Gallery), *Bananarama* (Really Creative Media, UK Tour), *Luv Esther* (UK Tour), *Gok Wan: Naked and Bearing all* (UK Tour), *Legally Blonde* (Korea/Monte Carlo), *Rudimental* (Really Creative Media, V Festival), *A Thousand Faces; Art Sung, Alma Maler* (Wilton's Music Hall), *Worst Wedding Ever* (Salisbury Playhouse), *Dracula* (Resorts World, Singapore), *The Island Nation* (Arcola Theatre), *Merch Yr Eog* (Theatre Genedlaethol), *Bugsy Malone*, *Legally Blonde* (Leicester Curve), *Ray Mears Tales Of Endurance, An Evening With Ray Mears* (UK Tour), *Box Of Photographs* (Polka Theatre), *Chwalfa* (Pontio), *Monster In The Maze* (Barbican), *Fugee & Wasted, Gods & Monsters* (Southwark Playhouse), *Merchant Of Venice* (Almedia Theatre), *Flashmob* (UK Tour), *The Waterbabies* (Ed Curtis), *The Prodigals* (The Belgrade), *Fallujah* (Cockpit Theatre), *The Handyman* (UK Tour), *1936* (Lilian Baylis Theatre), *Romeo & Juliet* (Headlong, National Tour), *Opera Holland Park* (Corporate Party), *Queen With Adam Lambert* (World Tour), *The Flying Dutchman* (English National Opera), *Aida* (Royal Albert Hall), *Straight To You Tour* (USA Tour), *Hairworld* (Paris). Content Manager (Nokia, Internal Web Video Communications).

Animator credits include: *Friendly Fires* (Really Creative Media, Brixton Academy), *Alice's Adventures Underground* (Vaults Festival), *The End Of Longing* (The Playhouse), *Pippin* (The Mernier Chocolate Factory), *Reasons To Be Cheerful* (Graeae and New Wolsey Theatre).

Thank Yous

Hasnain Abbas, Atri Banerjee, Satinder Chohan, Sharan Dhliwal, James Fritz, Jon Gilchrist, Humaira Iqbal, Hassan Joof, Rajiv Pattani, Hanne Schulpé (ASM week one), Nikesh Shukla, Kalungi Ssebandeke.

An Adventure Production Supporters

An Adventure has been made possible by a lead gift from Charles Holloway. The production is generously supported by the Peter Wolff Theatre Trust, Cockayne – Grants for the Arts and the London Community Foundation. We would also like to thank the Bush Theatre's Production Syndicate:

Inspired by India
Caro Millington

A New Life In Kenya
Catharine Brown
Matthew Byam Shaw
Simon Johnson
Philip Percival

A Future in England
Brian Smith

Bring Us Home
Clyde Cooper
Lesley Hill & Russ Shaw
Georgia Oetker
Susie Simkins

Productions are just one of the many areas you can support by making a donation to the Bush Theatre. To find out more about our patrons programme or other ways to support our work, please contact the Development Team on 020 8743 3584 or at development@bushtheatre.co.uk.

Bush Theatre

Bush Theatre, 7 Uxbridge Road, London W12 8LJ
Box Office: 020 8743 5050 | Administration: 020 8743 3584

Email: info@bushtheatre.co.uk
bushtheatre.co.uk
Alternative Theatre Company Ltd
(The Bush Theatre) is a Registered Charity and a company limited by guarantee.
Registered in England no. 1221968 Charity no. 270080

Bush
Theatre
We make theatre for London. Now.

The Bush is a world-famous home for new plays and an internationally renowned champion of playwrights. We discover, nurture and produce the best new writers from the widest range of backgrounds from our home in a distinctive corner of west London.

The Bush has won over 100 awards and developed an enviable reputation for touring its acclaimed productions nationally and internationally.

We are excited by exceptional new voices, stories and perspectives – particularly those with contemporary bite which reflect the vibrancy of British culture now.

Located in the newly renovated old library on Uxbridge Road in the heart of Shepherd's Bush, the theatre houses two performance spaces, a rehearsal room and the lively Library Bar.

Supported by
ARTS COUNCIL
ENGLAND

bushtheatre.co.uk

THANK YOU

The Bush Theatre would like to thank all its supporters whose valuable contributions have helped us to create a platform for our future and to promote the highest quality new writing, develop the next generation of creative talent and lead innovative community engagement work.

If you are interested in finding out how to be involved, please visit **bushtheatre.co.uk/support-us** or email **development@bushtheatre.co.uk** or call **020 8743 3584.**

An Adventure

Acknowledgements

An Adventure would not have happened without the Bush's investment in me as a writer from the very start of my career. The first extract of what would become my first play appeared at a scratch night here in 2012. That completed play would return for the Radar Festival in 2014, and Madani offered me my first ever commission the following year.

Developing and rehearsing this play at the Bush has given me some of the happiest and most artistically satisfying memories of my life. The people who work in this building are kind, passionate, funny, switched-on and hold no fear of a karaoke microphone. No matter where I go from here, the Bush will always be a large part of the story of where I came from.

Specific thank yous: Madani Younis, Omar Elerian and Stewart Pringle for shepherding the play from an excitable pitch to a (far too long) text.

Nyla Levy, Nitin Kundra, Joey Akubeze, Mona Goodwin for letting me hear the voices in this play for the first time.

Anjana Vasan, Shane Zaza and Anastasia Osei-Kuffour for making the characters live. Shubham Saraf, Aysha Kala, Nila Aalia, Selva Rasalingham and Martins Imhangbe for taking that journey forward with care and diligence.

Rosanna Vize, Ed Clarke, Sally Ferguson, Louise Rhodes-Brown, Anna Lewis, Lily O'Hara and Michael Ager for building a world. Eleanor Dear and Ana Carter for keeping that world running. Deborah Pugh for showing us how to move within it.

Jon Gilchrist for his unswerving, sometimes unnerving, enthusiasm.

Charles Holloway for taking a massive punt on me as a writer after seeing an extract of the play and the production supporters who made my vision a reality. I'll never forget that extraordinary generosity and I endeavour to pay it forward.

Deirdre O'Halloran for being patient with me when I would frequently tell her she was wrong, only to consistently realise five hours later that she was right.

Susan Wambui Kibaara, Mary Wanjiru Njoroge, Tayiana Chao and Olivia Windham Stewart for their assistance with names and their efforts to create a much needed Museum of British Colonialism.

Nikesh Shukla and the other Good Immigrants for making me feel proud and humbled in equal measure as well as audacious enough to believe that our stories are not only worth hearing but that they can speak across boundaries.

To my family for not always understanding what I do, but supporting it anyway, which – when you think about it – is harder than if they did know. Especially my sister, Shivani, for believing in me and making excuses on my behalf when I needed them.

Finally, to my grandparents – Kamla, Jyotibala, Rasiklal and Jayanthi: Thank you for being brave enough to strike out across the seas, thank you for loving me before I was even born, thank you for bringing me up as a man that I'm proud to be and thank you, most of all, for letting me stand on your shoulders long enough to find my own horizons.

NOTES

A note on dialogue

The dialogue is written mainly to reflect modern colloquial English. The performers should use their natural voices and inflect them only as directed by the text.

A note on pacing

The first act should be a rush.
The second act should be a quiver.
The third act should take its time.
None of it should feel like history.

A note on intention

Finally, this is a play of myth, of feeling, more than fact. In that spirit, stage directions can be altered or lost entirely. It is only necessary to understand that the aim of this piece is to encompass all the hopes and compromises, struggles and surrenders, emotions and echoes of a generation that crossed three continents before they were thirty, fighting diseases, war, hostile institutions, the sea itself and the pull of their own primal desires.

All so that their kids might become accountants.

One
1954–1959

1. Outskirts of Ahmedabad, India

A near-empty house.

A teenage girl. **Jyoti.** *Our heroine. She moves through the space with grace. This is her territory. She prepares the room, just as she likes it.*

She smells something in the air. Something coming. She sits.

A crack. A whoosh. The slam of torrential monsoon rain arriving uninvited.

A man arrives, dripping wet. Invited. But not by her. This is **Rasik.** *Early twenties. He sits down across from her, wipes his face with a handkerchief.*

Jyoti *holds up a picture.*

Jyoti   You look nothing like this.

Rasik   Really? I thought it was very –

Jyoti   Nope.

Rasik   Fair?

Jyoti   Nope.

Rasik   Oh.

Do I look better or worse?

Jyoti   Nuh uh, I ask the questions.

Rasik   Questions.

Jyoti   Yes, it's a little system I've put together, makes this shitshow more fun for me. All your lovely, desperate faces are laid out here, ranked top to bottom. Answer well, you move up, fuck me off, you move down. Simple!

Rasik And that's fun is it?

She points at some more photos in front of her on a table.

Jyoti I mean, the other 'suitors' were very keen . . .

I'll stick you in the middle, give you something to aim for.

She organises the photos into an order in front of her, top to bottom.

You can kick us off with a compliment if you like.

Rasik A compliment? Um ok uh . . .

Jyoti That hard huh?

Rasik No! Um . . .

Jyoti, you're a good-looking woman!

Jyoti Pft, come on that's not a compliment, Rasik, that's an objective statement of fact.

Rasik It is?

Jyoti Sure. My dad's lost all the money, most the land, the fields are dead, my family hasn't a drop of political power and yet there's still a gaggle of drooling men ready to throw me over their shoulder so. Stands to reason. I must be top-drawer fucking gorgeous. Whereas you . . .

She looks down at the photos.

. . . you're doing what you can. Respect.

Rasik Thanks.

Jyoti Heh I can't get over these photos. Such nervous faces! The same man took them?

Rasik Is that your first question or –

Jyoti He's *terrible*, who is this criminal?

Rasik A young English chap, very friendly. Only had a half hour, think he was on a break from his real job so it was a rush to get us all –

Jyoti What a scam! Get your money back if I was you.

Rasik It was your father that paid for him.

Jyoti Hah! That explains it, the tight bastard. Glad he's paying someone.

She looks at the photos again.

Mmm. It's not even 'nervous' is it? More a general air of . . .

Rasik Authority?

Jyoti Constipation. Would it hurt to break a smile for your future wife?

Rasik Oh see I wanted to smile, believe me, a smile suits my features really well actually.

Jyoti Uhuh.

Rasik But – and it's fascinating this – but apparently the old cameras, they take some time to work and the man said it's hard to hold a smile for long enough so . . .

He said a frown was the most noble expression I could reach for.

A pause as **Jyoti** *decides whether she believes it.*

Jyoti At least you're wearing a suit.

She starts to move **Rasik**'s *photo up the order.*

Rasik Of course!

She looks at the photo a little closer.

Jyoti Not yours though, is it?

Rasik Um . . . no it is mine of course/ it's mine –

Jyoti Doesn't fit. Big in the shoulders, short on the arms so it's either cheap or it's borrowed. Which would you rather I think?

Rasik *picks at his ill-fitting suit.*

Jyoti   You can tell me. I won't 'mark you down'.

Rasik *doesn't bite.*

You have the aura of a shrewd man, Rasik, too shrewd to waste your money on something you'll only wear once.

Rasik *thinks about lying but . . .*

Rasik   You're as sharp as they say.

Jyoti   Of course.

Rasik   It's borrowed, yes. But from someone whose auntie I helped move to Baroda and it's basically payment for that, so perhaps rented is a better way/to think –

Jyoti   A noble frown. A borrowed suit. And a British cut to boot. 'The perfect gentleman.' Is that what you're aiming for?

Rasik   I suppose.

Jyoti *shuffles the photos.* **Rasik**, *anxious, watches her do it.*

Jyoti   Right! Enough with the introductory bullshit, on to the nitty gritty! What do you do to pass the time?

Rasik   Erm. Work?

Jyoti   You must have some hobbies?

He coughs long, chesty and hard. **Jyoti** *winces. Starts to move his photo. He recovers. Tries to style it out.*

Rasik   Absolutely!

Sorry, hobbies, those are . . . ?

Jyoti   Do you read?

Rasik   I *can* read.

Jyoti   Is that what I asked?

Rasik   Newspapers. I read newspapers. I think it's important to stay up to date.

Jyoti   Oh God, you've got 'opinions' haven't you?

Rasik   Heh. Only the right ones!

Jyoti   Naturally. What man doesn't?

Jyoti *moves his photo lower.*

How about films? I adore films. American films, French films, Indian films also . . .

Rasik   Ah! Yes, me too, I like films very much!

Jyoti   Yeah? I saw *Amar* last week, have you seen *Amar?*

Rasik   No I haven't/but I want –

Jyoti   It's wonderful! See it's about this beautiful young woman who lives in a nice, big house with her widowed father. Sound familiar?

Rasik   That's you?

Jyoti   Exactly! It's me! Honestly, Rasik, you don't know how . . . how . . . invigorating it is to see your story on a screen that big!

Rasik   Can imagine. So what happens to the girl?

Jyoti   Didn't say she was a girl did I, I said she was a young woman.

Rasik   Of course. Forgive me –

Jyoti   A young woman . . .

Jyoti *leans in to the drama. Leans in to* **Rasik**.

Who falls . . . for a young man . . . !

Rasik   Oh classic story, beautiful story.

Jyoti   And with him she learns a lot about life and a lot about herself and she's really very happy about that.

Rasik *mirrors her lean.*

Rasik   Is that so?

Jyoti   Uhuh . . . but of course it goes terribly, terribly wrong!

She pulls away.

Rasik   Aw. How?

Jyoti   I'm not telling you, you have to pay for it. But it pulled at my heart, you know? Tell me, Rasik, what pulls at your heart?

Rasik   You mean apart from you?

Rasik *is no way smooth enough to pull off this line.* **Jyoti** *reaches for his photo.*

Sorry sorry sorry. Um.

Well . . . as I say, I do enjoy the films. But the thing is I haven't really

You know.

The money for them.

Jyoti   Oh.

A pause. She moves her hand to his photo again. He panics.

Rasik   Uh not just right now, I don't have it to hand is all! I've been saving it. For us. Priorities.

Jyoti   Of course.

Rasik   So like I –

To be clear, I *have* money, some money, yes, lots actually, we'll be going to the movies all the time, don't you worry about that!

Jyoti   Well I'd hope so or we're all just wasting our time here, aren't we!

She laughs – loud, long, goofy. Somewhere a baby starts to cry.

Jyoti (*Shouting.*)   Hey! Shanti!

She stands. Shouts again, off.

Jyoti   Shanti! It's doing it again!

She spins back around to face **Rasik**.

Sorry.

He points off.

Rasik   Are you not close to your sister?

Jyoti   Why makes you think that?

Rasik   How you were shouting . . .

Jyoti   She's fine, just . . .

Aggressively fertile.

Rasik   I see.

Jyoti   And she refuses to fuck off to her simpering husband's house, so he crawled into the walls here meaning she sits there, all day, just letting me know she can pump out a shitting, screaming machine, fresh out the tunnel, whenever she likes.

Rasik   They can't help it. They do that when they're young, cry all the time.

Jyoti   How would you know?

Rasik   Hey?

Jyoti   How would you know that? What makes you mister baby expert, mister?

Rasik   I'm not an expert I just –

Jyoti   You've had some kids of your own?

Rasik   No.

Jyoti   Been married already?

Rasik   God. No! No, not at all. I've got a lot of sisters. Brothers. All younger. I remember what they were like is all.

Jyoti   Right. But you've been with a woman?

A pause.

Have you ever been with a woman, Rasik?

A huge pause.

'Cause twenty-two is old isn't it? It's old for a man to be getting married. Definitely old to be marrying a woman of sixteen.

Rasik   Right. Yes, I suppose it is. Old.

Jyoti   So old I assume that any sort of man worth the label has at the very least found himself in a dark alley on a dark night with a hole in his heart, blood in his loins and some dim lady that he's paid too little for. But perhaps you don't have money for that hobby either?

Rasik *reaches for an answer. Doesn't find one.* **Jyoti** *moves his photo down.*

Rasik   Is that the bottom?

Jyoti   Where you are? Yep, that's the bottom.

Rasik   Oh.

Jyoti   Sorry.

Rasik   Don't apologise, it's your choice to make.

Jyoti   Mmm choice yes, that's an odd way of putting it. A choice between content, not form. Not 'do you want these bastards?' just 'which of these bastards do you want?'

Rasik   That's still choice. To have any choice at all is power in this world. And heh, if you like us all you could even just –

No.

Jyoti   What?

Rasik   Never mind.

Jyoti   I could what?

A beat. **Rasik** *reluctant to spit it out but . . .*

Rasik   You could choose to be like Draupadi?

Jyoti   Draupadi. Like the Pandavas Draupadi?

Rasik   Yeah.

Jyoti   You're suggesting I marry all five of you?

Rasik   Less a suggestion and more something/to think about –

Jyoti   Ok, listen, dickhead, let's be super clear about this. I don't want *one* husband, so bolting on how-many-the-fuck-of-you there are won't suddenly make it a good idea, especially since – frankly – none of you have been particularly inspiring, no stories to light up a marquee, so if you've got anything magical to pull out the bag now would be the time.

He considers.

Rasik   I –

My mother says I have many fine virtues?

Jyoti *puts her head in her hands.*

For example, I don't drink. Never have. Not a single drop!

Jyoti   That's a virtue?

Rasik   You'd prefer your husband to drink?

Jyoti   God yes. Wouldn't you?

A beat.

Rasik   I mean. I could try it?

Jyoti   Wow! Your virtues didn't last long there, friend.

Rasik   Well it's a compromise, isn't it, marriage?

Jyoti *stares at him. Nods to herself.*

She reaches down, pulls out a bottle of whisky, slams it on the table.

Jyoti   Prove it.

Rasik   That's yours?

Jyoti   Sort of. It's how Dad keeps things ticking along.

She unscrews it, takes a sip, hands it to **Rasik**.

He makes it in the bath, then sells it to the drunks down by the river. I say river, this is the only thing that flows down there.

Drain it, please.

Rasik   All of it?

Jyoti   Yes.

Rasik   That whole bottle.

Jyoti   Yep.

Rasik   I can't manage that.

Jyoti   Fine. A compromise. Half.

Rasik *looks at it. Hesitates.*

Jyoti   What, you're too good for my family's hospitality, Rasik?

Rasik   No . . .

Jyoti   So you're some secret Muslim then?

Rasik   That doesn't mean anything, Muslims drink.

Jyoti   They're not supposed to.

Rasik   Jinnah, the most famous Muslim of our time, he drank. A lot.

A beat.

Jyoti   Did he?

Rasik   Yep. And he loved a ham sandwich.

Jyoti   Hah, he never! How do you know that?

Rasik *smiles. He senses a hook at last.*

Rasik Newspapers.

She looks him up and down. Takes the bottle back from him.
Has a sip.

Jyoti You look a bit like him in that suit. So Western!

Rasik Yeah? I liked Jinnah!

Rasik *looks at the bottle, takes a tentative sip.*

Jyoti Tsk. Careful, Rasik. Don't let papa hear you say that about a Pakistani . . .

Rasik Hey, Jinnah was first and foremost a Gujarati!
Sort of.

He hands the bottle back to **Jyoti**. *They sip and exchange as they*
go on.

Jyoti But he's not an Indian and that's all that matters.

Rasik He *was* Indian.

Jyoti Ok so he was Indian and then he wasn't?

Rasik I guess you would say that he was born Indian and died Pakistani?

Jyoti Right. But still Gujarati?

Rasik Erm yes I suppose. And Muslim too, still that.

Jyoti A Gujarati Muslim ex-Indian Western-suit-wearing Pakistani who liked a drink . . .

Rasik . . . and a ham sandwich.

Jyoti And a ham bloody sandwich!

Rasik Perfect!

They laugh, look at each other. This might work after all.

I'm not either, you know.

Jyoti You're not what?

Rasik Indian. I was born in Kenya (*he pronounces it Keen-ya*).

Jyoti Huh! That's so cool!

Rasik You think so? That's not what most people say.

Jyoti Why, what do those idiots say?

Rasik Call us janglies – jungle people. There's no love for me here.

Rasik *wrings out his handkerchief.* **Jyoti** *smiles, puts her hand on his photo.*

Jyoti There could be.

Rasik, *gripping the handkerchief, looks up slowly, hopefully.*

Yeah, I think it's probably down to two.

She sweeps the other photos from the table. Picks up two.

You and this guy.

Jyoti *turns the photo to him.* **Rasik**'s *face crumples.*

Rasik Kirit Kumar.

Jyoti You know him? He was here just before you.

Rasik I bet he was.

Jyoti And he has his own suit. It's really nice.

Rasik I bet it is!

Jyoti He must have loads! In fact, you know Kirit Kumar's father is building a suit factory? The other side of town. Says Ahmedabad is made for it, the perfect combination of great workmen and –

Rasik Poor exploited fools more like . . .

A beat. **Jyoti** *realises . . .*

Jyoti Ahhh! He lent you the suit you're wearing, didn't he?

It's true. **Rasik** *rushes to deflect.*

Rasik   The thing about Kirit Kumar is –

See Kirit Kumar has – heh.

Look, I can tell you some things about Kirit Kumar, things Kirit Kumar wouldn't want you to know!

Jyoti   Like what?

A beat. **Rasik** *uncertain.*

You want this, Rasik, you're so close, so don't pretend you care about your friend and tell me, you want to tell me.

A beat.

Rasik   He's a pisser.

Jyoti   What's a pisser?

Rasik   A guy who pisses himself. What else?

Jyoti   Is that true? That's not true . . .

Rasik   Find out in your marital bed if you like.

Jyoti   Ew.

Rasik   Whereas I'm active. I'm strong. I'm young.

Jyoti   Ish.

Rasik   With full bladder control and when it comes down to it, I think you want a man who will warm your bed with his body, not his urine.

Jyoti *paces. Plays with the two photos.*

Jyoti   Oooh. This is tough! Going to need one last question.

Rasik   Hit me.

A beat.

Jyoti   How long will you live?

Rasik   What?

Jyoti   Do you have an expectation of the years you have left?

A beat.

Rasik   Um, get to seventy? That seems reasonable.

Jyoti   Seventy! Ok, so you're nearly a third through already. I've got my whole life ahead of me, why should I go with a man who's a third done with his? A man with no prospects, a man I'm sure my father suggested as a joke or a favour, I don't know, he has all sorts of reasons/for what he –

Rasik   Typhoid.

Jyoti   Not a great offer, that.

Rasik   No. My family. My brothers and sisters. I was looking after them. That's why I'm behind. But they died anyway so –

A pause.

Jyoti   How many?

Rasik   Nine.

Jyoti   And they –

Rasik   Yep. I watched every single one of them go.

Jyoti *takes this in.*

Jyoti   What were they called?

Rasik *doesn't answer.*

You want sympathy?

Rasik *stares at her.*

Rasik   Never. I never want that. Not from you, not from anyone!

A pause. The bitterness sits with him. And then . . . something begins to stir . . .

You asked why I'm here? That's why. I want to trade a shitty past for a tolerable present.

Jyoti   'Something to aim for'?

Rasik   Someone to be better for. And who wouldn't want to be better for a woman like you?

Rasik *means it. He's finding his voice.*

Don't think I'm not ashamed. I'm not the prospect I should be, but I swear to you, Jyoti, pick me and I will make *us* – the decision that you make here right now – the very best decision you ever make over your whole long life, the greatest adventure you could ever have. You could marry a Kirit, you could get used to sitting on your arse, paying with other people's money . . .

Jyoti   I quite like other people's money.

Rasik   . . . and there's a life in that, sure. But I know how to think, how to learn, and I can tell you want that too so I'll always have something new to give you, things money can't give you, like . . .

He stands. Points off.

That car outside! It's rusting, it's not moved in, what, months?

Jyoti   Years. We can't afford a driver anymore.

Rasik   I can drive, I've done it for supposedly better men. You could go wherever you wanted, whenever you wanted.

Jyoti   You'd be my lover and my chauffeur?

Rasik   Better. I'll teach you to do it yourself.

The . . . the chauffeur part not the lover –

Jyoti   Hah!

Rasik   Also that! That right there! I'll make you laugh every day, every single day of your life!

Rasik *feeling the momentum, sweeps up the bottle of whisky.*

And best of all? Best of all? I'm a flexible guy!

He looks at **Jyoti** *like he's a hero for the ages, steps up onto his chair and then necks half of it in one go.*

Jyoti   Wow.

Rasik   Ugh.

Jyoti   Wow.

Rasik   It burns.

Jyoti   Yeah.

I mean he *did* make it in the bath. I *did* tell you that.

Rasik   It won't stop burning.

Jyoti   No one's ever actually done that you know.

Rasik (*Gasping.*)   What?

Jyoti   The others, they all refused to do it because they're not crazy.

Rasik   Well. Here I am. The crazy man in the good suit.

Jyoti   No one said it was good.

Rasik   But I *look* good in it right? I look good and I know things. I know that the future is anywhere but India, this country will devour its youth. So we'll build our own world. Our own future. For us. For our kids.

Jyoti   Steady on.

Rasik   And we'll see the most wondrous places – Paris, New York, Blackpool!

Jyoti   Blackpool?

Rasik   The photographer, he says it's the *only* place to be these days. Even Frank Sinatra goes to Blackpool!

Jyoti   Wow.

Something terrible occurs inside of **Rasik**.

Rasik   But the only place I'm going right now is your garden so I can throw up the contents of that bottle along with my dignity and I don't think I can face coming back once I'm done so I was wondering if you could please give me something, Jyoti.

Anything?

Jyoti   Yeah.

She smiles. Pushes Kirit Kumar's photo off the desk. Picks up **Rasik**'s.

You'll do.

2. Dandi Beach, India

The west coast. **Jyoti** *and* **Rasik** *on the shore. It's hot. It's bright. They squint.*

Jyoti   Where?

Rasik   There. That way.

Jyoti   I don't see anything.

Rasik   You wouldn't. Unless one of your many gifts is the ability to see over four thousand kilometres of water.

Jyoti   God. There's so much of it.

Rasik   That's the point of the sea, makes you think twice about leaving the land.

Jyoti   Won't stop *us* though, eh?

Rasik   I'm telling you, Jyoti, the air over there is clearer, the sun is warmer, the whole world just feels like it's waiting for you to be whoever you want. And one day we'll be standing on a beach, our old, cracked feet deep in the Kenyan sand, looking back this way. Proud of who we are.

Jyoti   I can't wait, absolutely cannot wait!

She toes the water.

Rasik   We should head back soon. Your father will be worried.

Jyoti   Oh fuck my dad, we just got here.

Rasik   It'll be dark soon, you won't like driving when it's dark.

Jyoti   Then I'll just drive faster.

We've come all this way, we're not heading home yet! We're going in.

Rasik   In the sea? But.

Jyoti   But what? Don't you know how to swim?

Rasik *doesn't reply.* **Jyoti** *smiles at him.*

Well you better hold on to me then, hadn't you.

She goes in, pulls him with her.

Rasik   Jyoti!

Rasik *freaks out. Splashes frantically.* **Jyoti** *laughs at him.*

Jyoti   Chill out, Tarzan, your toes can still touch the ground.

Rasik   Tarzan?!

Jyoti   Yeah, I've decided that's my nickname for you, he's a jungle person too. *King* of the jungle no less.

She stops swimming, nods to the water: 'See? Not that deep.'

Rasik *stops struggling. His feet touch the ground. He relaxes a little.*

Rasik   No further than here though.

Jyoti   Nope! We're going further, my friend! Do you want to climb onto my back? I'll carry you.

Rasik   Hah.

Jyoti   I'm not joking. You really need to learn when I'm joking if this is going to work out, Rasik.

Rasik *stares at her.*

The water will carry you. It'll take the weight.

He looks around.

No-one's here.

A beat. He slowly climbs onto her back. It's a more complicated manoeuvre than it should be. But they pull it off. They wade in further.

Rasik   This is nice.

Jyoti   Mmmhmm.

They look out sea. They enjoy the nice.

Rasik   Jyoti.

Jyoti   Mhm?

Rasik   You should know.

The boat that left last week . . .

Jyoti   For Mombasa?

Rasik   Headed for Mombasa, but didn't reach Mombasa.

A beat.

Jyoti   Wait.

So that means . . . ?

Rasik   Yep. He's dead.

Jyoti   Kirit Kumar cannot be dead, people like him don't just die.

Rasik   His mother heard last night. Four days out of Porbunder. Apparently he didn't even make it off the ship.

Jyoti   Oh my God.

Rasik   Horrible. Couldn't swim, see.

Jyoti   God.

Rasik   Just horrible.

Jyoti   Yes.

A solemn pause.

And surprising, when you consider that he's used to being surrounded by liquid.

Rasik *takes a moment to get the joke. He tries to contain himself.*

Jyoti   Are you laughing?

Rasik   No. Dreadful what you said. Pure evil.

Jyoti   You're laughing though.

Rasik   No I'm –

He gives up holding it in. Starts to laugh.

She leans up to kiss him. He leans into it.

Rasik   That was so cheesy.

Jyoti   Hey!

Rasik   Did you see that in one of your cinema films?

Jyoti   Shut up!

She turns away from him and looks out to sea again.

Rasik   My wife, the young seductress at wild, taking vulnerable men in the middle of the ocean. How many wandering sailors have been lost to Jyoti's charms?! Aaaagghh!

He feigns drowning. **Jyoti** *remains silent.*

Rasik   Are you OK? I was joking, only joking.

A beat.

Jyoti   I'm going to miss you.

Rasik   It's only a year or so, that's nothing. And the violence! It's still dangerous.

Jyoti   I like dangerous.

Rasik   Not this kind of dangerous. Too dangerous for you.

Jyoti   Too dangerous for *me*? You threw your back out getting into the car.

Rasik   What I mean is I know it. I know that place. Those people. How to handle the situation.

He settles his hands on her head. Kisses her on it.

Trust me, by the time you come over, it'll all have calmed down, I will have set the foundations, we'll do everything I promised, as I promised, and you'll never want to come back. We'll never *have* to come back.

A beat. **Jyoti** *smiles at* **Rasik**.

Jyoti   I want you to touch me, Rasik. Will you touch me?

He, industrially, slaps his hands on her arms. She looks at them with disdain.

That's not what I meant.

She looks at him, willing him to find the meaning.

Rasik   Oh?

Oh! Here? Will that be –

Good? For you?

Jyoti *sighs*.

Jyoti   I'm selling it by the way. The car.

Rasik   What?

Jyoti   I'm selling it and I want you to take the money with you.

Rasik   Won't your family need that? Your sister?

Jyoti   Where's she going to want to go? She'd need some basic curiosity first.

Rasik   No, Jyoti, no I couldn't –

Jyoti   Quit with the false modesty. Accept the money. Just make it worth it, that's all I ask. For now though? You can give me a present in return.

She winks at him. **Rasik** *looks mortified.*

I'm not expecting you to reinvent the good fuck here, Rasik. I know you're nervous, just give it your best shot.

Rasik   Heh. Sure thing, boss.

They smile suggestively at each other. **Rasik** *turns to shore.*

But Tarzan needs his feet on the ground for that.

3. Nairobi Slums, Kenya

Outside a shanty hut.

Rasik *holds a camera, a Polaroid Land Model 95. He stands in front of* **David***, late twenties, who's eating his breakfast.*

Rasik   You're Wachira? David?

His speech is ever-so-slightly more refined.

David   Yes, I am David Wachira.

Rasik   And that's your real name? Your birth name?

David   Who would call *themselves* David?

Rasik   No I mean –

David   Do you have a problem with Davids?

Rasik   No.

David   Did a David spit in your milk once?

Rasik   My apologies sir, it's nothing. Just to confirm, these are your lodgings, Mr . . . Wachira.

David   'Lodgings.'

Rasik   Place of residence.

David   I know what lodgings are, mister. Yes, they're mine.

Rasik   Ok, well if you could just stand right there in front of . . .

David   My lodgings?

Rasik   Yes. So I can see you and the building, sir.

David *steps into place. He's having a great time.* **Rasik** *is not.*

That'll do.

He raises the camera. **David** *holds up his hand.*

David   Hey! Do I smile?

Rasik   Not if you don't want to.

David   I'd like to. I like to smile.

Rasik   Whatever you feel like, sir.

David *smiles.*

David   They sent you because you're Asian?

Rasik *avoids* **David***'s smile.*

They did, didn't they? Out into the slums, amongst the fellow savages.

A beat. **Rasik***, unable to hold it in anymore, looks right at* **David***.*

Rasik   'Wachira', that's –

David   Yes?

Rasik   Kikuyu? Isn't it? It's a Kikuyu name?

David *gives him a look. Hadn't expected that.*

David   Well spotted.

Rasik   But –

David That's not possible. That's what you're going to say. Because the army . . .

Rasik The army swept through here. Because of what the Mau Mau rebels did in Lari. They told me at the briefing, about the massacre. So the army swept through Nairobi and they took all the Kikuyu away.

David Right! So I can't be Kikuyu.

Rasik Guess not.

David Or maybe what you've heard isn't the whole story. Maybe not all Kikuyu are Mau Mau. Maybe some are on the side of the government and are grateful that those madmen are nearly on their knees. So what am I do you think? A madman? A loyalist? A ghost?

Rasik Not my job to say, sir.

He points at the camera.

I should . . .

David Of course.

Rasik Ready? And one, two and –

David Wait wait wait wait. This is official government business.

He drops the smile into a serious face.

Perhaps we should be more official about it.

David *gestures to continue, then drops his hands to his side, soldier straight.*

Rasik *hits the camera shutter. A photo comes out the front.*

David Can I see?

Rasik I suppose you –

David *grabs the photo.*

David There's nothing there.

Rasik   It takes a little –

David *begins to shake the photo.*

And um, it's actually – heh you don't need to do that.

David   Huh?

He starts to blow on the picture.

Rasik   It doesn't have to dry, it's a chemical process, so you don't have to –

David *shakes the photo again, harder.*

You know what, it's fine.

Rasik *checks his camera lens for dust. A beat.*

So you're not.

He drops into a whisper.

Are you . . . ?

David   A rebel? Rebels are reckless. Divisive! That's how mistakes like Lari happen. I'm a responsible man. I do what's best for my country.

David *stares at the photo unsatisfied.*

What about *you*?

Rasik   Am *I* a rebel or . . . ?

David   Are you here to fight? Said in the newspaper a little while back, this man from England, the colonial secretary, Mr Oliver . . . Oliver . . . I can't remember his name but they said a delegation of Asians asked to fight the Mau Mau and the colonial secretary gave his approval, they're calling up men right now, I see them marching. So. Tell me.

Have you come to kill my countrymen?

A beat.

Rasik   I am your countrymen, Mr Wachira. I was born right here.

David, *intrigued, hands the photo back to* **Rasik**.

David   In Nairobi?

Rasik   Yes, my father was a station master near here a long time ago.

David   Huh! Which station?

Rasik   Kijabe.

David   Kijabe . . . Kijabe. Ooof! That's far!

Rasik   Well –

David   That's not near, mister, that's a looooong way from Nairobi, *my* father was on those trains.

Rasik   Really?

David   Oh yes! We were a proud farming family once and when the whites pushed us off our land, he didn't push back, gave it all up to feed coal into the burners, hoping they'd let him drive their little locomotive some day. Idiot. Was tough. Him being away so much. Tough for you too, eh?

Rasik   Maybe a little better. My dad said the worst part was that he could only talk to the station either side of him but either side of him the stations were run by bloody Patels.

David   My God! Poor man!

Rasik   I know.

David   Those guys are so boring!

Rasik   *So* boring!

David   And now you're back, hoping to do better than Daddy, but instead, bam! You've really landed yourself in the shit! I mean, talk about bad timing! State of emergency, these bad, mad Kikuyu running around causing trouble with their Embu and Meru pals, all for their silly freedom!

A beat.

What department did you say you work for?

Rasik   Public Works.

David   Public Works! See, that's funny, isn't it? You're a member of the public. Do you think the public works work for you?

Rasik   Well we're trying to –

David   It doesn't work for me. It's not working for us, any of us. You have kids?

Rasik   Not yet. Soon I hope.

David   And you'll do your best for them?

Rasik   Yes.

David   You'll bring them up in Nairobi?

Rasik   Yes.

David   As Indians?

Rasik   No.

David   Kenyans?

Rasik   Yes.

David   Proud Kenyans. Free Kenyans.

Rasik   Yes.

David   You have dreams for them.

Rasik   Absolutely. Who we make our dreams for, that's the only decision we really get to make.

David   I dream that my children will rule this land. Not much to ask.

Rasik   No.

A beat. **Rasik** *holds the photo out to* **David.**

It's a good one. Captures your eyes.

David *looks at it. He likes this photo.*

I think it *could* work.

David   Eh?

Rasik   It doesn't work yet, you're right. But I think it could. If you're interested?

David *looks back up to* **Rasik**. *He likes this man too.*

4. Nairobi Suburbs, Kenya

Jyoti *and* **Rasik**'*s house. Humble, but cosy. Just after dinner.*

Jyoti, *unpacking suitcases, is across from* **David**, *who's laughing.*

Jyoti   It's not funny.

David   It's a little bit funny. So it was your money?

Jyoti   Stop laughing and help me with these.

She points **David** *to the suitcases.*

Jyoti   I can't believe he didn't tell you.

David   Your husband's a proud man!

Jyoti   He's a fucking dead man is what he is.

Rasik *enters, carrying three glasses of whisky in hand.*

Rasik   Who's a dead man?

David   You didn't tell me you used your wife's money to buy our farm.

Rasik   I like to think it was both our money.

Rasik *hands a drink to both* **Jyoti** *and* **David**.

Jyoti   You were meant to use it to find us a nice place to live.

Rasik   No, you said to make it worth it, and I have. I've made an investment. Land. Nothing better than that.

David   But it's given *me* a nice place to live, so guess you're my landlord, Jyoti?

Jyoti *looks embarrassed.* **David** *opens one of the suitcases.*

Oh these are sweet!

David *holds up some baby clothes.*

Bit small for you eh, Rasik?

Jyoti   Think all of it will be, by the looks of him.

Rasik   Hey!

David   Yes, he's gotten fat, hasn't he?

Rasik   I *am* right here.

David   I know, Big Man, we couldn't have missed you!

Jyoti *and* **David** *laugh. Share the tiniest look.*

Jyoti   Those are my sister's off-casts. Thought they could be a nice gift.

A beat. **David** *inspects the baby clothes.*

David   I'll take them. Some of the women in the forest, they could use –

Rasik *gives* **David** *a silencing look.*

Jyoti   Forest? Why are they in the forest?

Rasik   David's got friends all over.

David   Some prefer it to living in the Reserves, that's all. Wambui just had a little boy. She could use these.

Rasik   Well. Have them, why not . . .

David *looks to* **Jyoti**. *She nods. He looks around.*

David   I like what you've done here.

Jyoti   Thank you.

David   Five minutes and you've made this place look better than he managed in a year.

Jyoti   A year and a *half*. And what can I say, I'm a genius with my hands, furnishings, fashion, food, you name it, whereas Rasik . . . suddenly all about the knives and forks. I was not ready for that . . .

Rasik   A useful skill for particular occasions.

David   He's learning to be a good boy for lovely Mr Stephens!

Jyoti   His boss?

David   His role model.

Rasik   He's a decent man. One of the good ones.

David   Yes, if he promoted me all the time I'd think he was pretty great, too.

Rasik   Only so far.

David   Further than I'd get . . .

Jyoti   Because you're black?

An awkward pause. **David** *looks to* **Rasik**.

David   Because he likes them tubby.

Jyoti *laughs.* **Rasik** *scowls, gestures for them to sit.*

Rasik   It's all your beer that's done this to me.

Jyoti   You drink beer now too! God, this is a lot to take in . . .

David   You know, miss, he's got all these airs, but he's trouble. When I first saw him I admit I thought 'who's this chickenshit the British have sent me this time?' but then two days later he's back, asking me to come with him, to look at some land . . .

Jyoti   The farm.

David   Yes! And so we head up together, up near Kamiti, he wears his smartest suit, I'm in his spare, barely fits . . .

Jyoti   You have *two* suits now . . . ?

Rasik *looks embarrassed.*

David   And I sit in the car as he goes into this old barn, squatting on this neglected, shabby patch of land and my God, not even five minutes later, he's shaking hands on the porch with this poor farmer, who's just staring at me, clearly he's been spooked by the Mau Mau . . .

Jyoti   That's . . . the rebels?

Rasik   She doesn't need to hear this.

David   . . . and then Rasik swaggers back to the car and says . . .

What did you say? 'Mr David . . .'

Rasik *sighs. Continues.*

Rasik   'Mr David, have you ever been to the Palace Hotel?'

David   Ah yes! 'It's only up the road and we need to celebrate!'

And you know, I haven't done that, I've haven't been to the Palace Hotel, because the Palace is for whites only.

Rasik   Not anymore . . .

David   The sign's still hanging there.

Rasik   It's an old sign.

Jyoti   Shut up, Rasik, you're ruining the story!

David   . . . and so we pull up, go in, still in our suits . . .

Jyoti *is enthralled.*

Jyoti   And then?

David   And then we get to the bar, no one's said anything, there's gawping of course but no one does a damn thing and then Rasik comes out with.

Rasik   'We'll have two bottles of –'

David *nudges him.*

David   No no, do the voice! He did a fabulous voice!

Rasik *clears his throat, and approximating a refined English accent . . .*

Rasik   'We'll have two bottles of your finest Tusker please!' It's a locally made beer.

David   Locally made by foreigners.

Jyoti   Right . . .

David   And you wouldn't believe the place could get any quieter but . . .

He gestures to indicate total silence.

Rasik   I was happy to leave at this point.

David   He was! All his cockiness drained out of him, but I held our hero firm and you know what they did? They served us!

Jyoti   Yes!

David   They gave us our bottles, I gave them our shillings, raised my beer and told those silent faces . . .

David *raises his glass,* **Jyoti** *joins in enthusiastically,* **Rasik** *less so.*

'Hey! We're your new neighbours! You can see a little of us now if you're nice, or a lot of us later if you're not!'

Jyoti   Hah! Sounds dangerous.

Rasik   Like I said, I got carried away, it won't be happening again.

David   Ahh see missus, he'll stop these antics for you.

Jyoti   Oh he shouldn't stop if he doesn't want to.

She looks at **Rasik**, *admiringly. A beat.*

I just hope he handles beer better than his liquor is all.

Rasik *groans in recognition.*

David   Hah!

Rasik   Ok, no more stories tonight.

Jyoti   That's a shame, I'd love to hear about what possessed you to buy a farm when you haven't even managed to keep your house plants alive.

Rasik   David's people sort it, they know this soil.

David   The British won't let us buy it, but we know what to do with it.

Rasik   Whereas we have a little more favour, we can do a little better.

David   Now does that seem fair to you, Jyoti?

Jyoti   Not at all.

Rasik   Don't drag her into this.

Jyoti   It's disgusting in fact.

David   Too right.

Rasik   She doesn't know the first thing about it.

Jyoti   Hey!

Rasik   What? It's true.

David   Maybe an outsider has the best perspective.

Rasik   You're not giving her perspective. Now, I admit it's not the best system . . .

David   Very generous!

Rasik   . . . yet the world always moves towards justice.
Slower than is convenient. But by this time next year, they'll
have passed a law allowing land ownership for all Kenyans, I
swear on my life.

David   I do love you when you're in an Establishment
mood, Rasik . . .

Rasik   You know what. We're not doing this now. Who
wants a top up?

Jyoti   Hang on . . .

Rasik   They've understood that they were wrong and
they'll make it right, that's all I'm saying.

Jyoti   So, what, you think they just woke up one day and
realised they were awful? Nothing to do with trying to stop
the uprising.

Rasik   No I –

Jyoti   If only someone told Mr Gandhi that the British
eventually figure it out themselves, would've saved him a lot
of effort.

Rasik *sighs, disapproving of the on-going conversation.*

Rasik   The 'uprising' is failing. Ask David, he's had his
sympathies with the Mau Mau, but he's smart enough to
plan for a future beyond all this gunplay. Aren't you, David?

David   The farm. It's a start.

Rasik   You have to come see it, Jyoti, it's beautiful, the
height of the harvest. The life springing from that earth is a
symbol that one day this country will work for all of us, all
our children, Asian, black and –

David   Not the whites. Not them.

A beat. **Jyoti** *scans both men's faces.*

Rasik   Naturally, they'll have to give up power but then
eventually –

David   There will never be a place for the wazungu in this country. The sooner they're gone the better for us.

Rasik   Uh they built this city . . . .

David   Nobody asked them to.

Rasik   Heh. I can tell from that look that you think I'm disagreeing with you, David, I'm not, I'm honestly not, I'm saying don't make India's mistake. Independence is coming, the key is in the door, the opening is inevitable but if you force it, SNAP! it's chaos, everyone suffers . . .

David   Not everyone. Our descendants will thank us for clearing out the weeds.

A tense beat.

Jyoti   Just to say, while we're on it. I'm not clearing out any fucking weeds.

The men laugh, despite themselves. Tension broken.

David   And you left this woman behind, Rasik!

Rasik   I didn't *leave* her . . .

Jyoti   He bloody did! With my sister and her horde.

Rasik   You're being a little unkind.

Jyoti   You think so? Then you're welcome to go back and be the wet-nurse. Your tits are certainly getting big enough.

David   Oof!

Jyoti *sees* **Rasik**'s *annoyance, realises she's gone a bit far but –*

Jyoti   Make that face all you like, I'm not saying sorry.

David   I think that's my cue to go.

Jyoti   So soon?

David   Lots to do before morning.

He holds up the baby clothes, shares a knowing look with **Rasik**.

Must get these to Wambui. Lovely to meet you, Jyoti. I'll see you soon.

He makes his exit. **Jyoti** *turns to* **Rasik.**

Jyoti Are you mad at me? You look like you're mad at me.

Rasik No just. David. If you get him going, he never shuts up. That's all.

Jyoti Uhuh. Well I have a question if that's ok. Two questions in fact. One, will these 'arrangements' get you into trouble?

Rasik Of course not.

Jyoti Because I didn't wait this long just to see you get locked up.

Rasik It's all above board, I promise.

Jyoti Two . . . this isn't a question, actually, this is a statement.

I wasn't joking, I'm not working on any bastard farm.

Rasik Hah! Well, either way. I'm glad you're here with me at last.

Jyoti *smiles at him.*

Jyoti It's a little exciting isn't it! 'Investments.' Giving it to The Man! You're actually making it happen.

Rasik No, *we're* making it happen. And this is just the start.

Jyoti Yeah.

I like your tits. So you know. They suit you.

Rasik Thanks.

They share a look. Both in on the joke. Mutual admiration. Mutual thrill.

You can have a closer look if you like?

5. Outskirts of Nairobi, Kenya

The farm. **David** *holds up a film poster.*

Jyoti, *pregnant, sits in front of him, holding a metal container. She seems distracted.*

David   'Weird, mysterious love rites.'

Jyoti   Sounds good to me . . .

David   'Performed by sex-mad natives.'

Jyoti   Who would've guessed?

David   'Cult secrets of barbaric people practising BLACK. MAGIC!' Hands up, who told them about the black magic? Guys?

Jyoti   Not me sir, not me.

David   'Filmed in Africa in Flaming Colour.' Very sensual. That part's true at least.

He rips the poster in two.

You know what this is? This is a declaration of victory. They think they can tell their tales about who we are. And people were queuing around the block for this rubbish!

Jyoti   Awful. Although . . .

David   What?

Jyoti   I mean.

You're not Mau Mau are you? It's not your problem.

David   A black body on a white screen. It's my problem whether I'm looking for it or not.

A beat.

Jyoti   Will Rasik be back soon you think? (*Gesturing to the container.*) This will get cold.

David   Probably. Irrigation surveys are the only thing more boring than him.

A beat.

Jyoti   You think he's boring?

David   Boring has a charm to it.

Are you alright? You look –

Jyoti   I'm fine.

David   Was I being a bit –

Jyoti   Not at all . . .

David   Just. Find it hard, seeing that in my city . . .

Jyoti   No, of course. I understand.

A beat.

David   The baby? It's tough huh? You probably shouldn't be coming out here in this heat, Rasik can bring his own lunches. Hell, he should skip a few!

Jyoti   No. I mean yes. It is tough, sometimes I just want to grab my belly and . . .

Can I just ask cause it's been bugging me. Why do you have that crate?

David   Which crate?

Jyoti   Uhh the crate full of guns?

A beat.

In the barn. I was looking for somewhere to leave the food, before you came back and I found the crate . . .

David   Guns in a crate! Huh. I'll have to ask the boys . . .

Jyoti   David . . .

David   Must be for safety. Get all sorts around here after dark.

Jyoti   Please don't treat me like an idiot.

You're with them aren't you? The rebels.

David *thinks about playing dumb. Sees it's not worth it. His silence tells all.*

I see. And Rasik –

David   Rasik doesn't know. He thinks I help them from time to time, but we don't talk about it. I imagine he thinks it's cute, keeping up the struggle, David's little hobby. But the guns. He doesn't know about those.

Jyoti   Why do you have to bring them *here*?

David   Access to the forest. Where our camps are. You can't make it from the city anymore, too many patrols. But they're not watching the farms.

Jyoti *thinks on this.*

Jyoti   It could get us into trouble.

David   It won't. We only move when it's dark, the British don't have a clue.

Do you want money?

Jyoti   What?

David   To keep quiet. We're not as broken as they say . . .

A beat.

Jyoti   Look at your eyes.

David   What?

Jyoti   You're enjoying this. Playing the hero. I mean why not, running around with guns, that's more fun than making peace, more fun than talking.

David   Talking!

Jyoti   Like Mr Kenyatta! He's one of your leaders isn't he?

David Oh you know so much suddenly! Reading Rasik's old newspapers, huh?

Jyoti Not everything I do is about Rasik. He's not my fucking dad. Got that?

David *raises his hands: 'Ok.'*

David Kenyatta. He's Kikuyu. But he isn't Mau Mau. He speaks against us, every chance he can and you know what's funny? The British insisted he was one of us anyway and now he does his talking from jail. That's where peaceful ways get you when the powerful own the peace.

A beat.

Jyoti Have you though? Have you actually killed anyone?

An uncomfortable pause.

David You don't need to be scared of me, Jyoti.

Jyoti I'm not scared of you.

David I haven't laid a finger on any Asians. In fact, those guns? Made by a Sikh, a blacksmith, in the middle of town! We're on the same side here.

Jyoti But you *have* killed people.

A beat. He's drawn by her curiosity.

David It was the army the first time. King's African Rifles in the war. They sent us up to Gondar, you know it?

Jyoti *shakes her head. He sits by her.*

North of here. Ethiopia, the Italians had it. When they told us that's where we were going, I was pleased. They'd been sending planes, the Italians, strafing our children, my sisters, my brothers, on their way to school. Those filthy fascists, I was so ready to return their bullets back to them! For the three days it took us to get there, I pictured every detail of the moment I'd do it, the look on the man's face as I raised my rifle, how all of his blood would run out of it, squirm back off home, leave him paler than he already was.

When we arrived, the fighting was already vicious, the city burning and I don't know why I hadn't thought of it but the Italians, they had their own askaris, local soldiers. Like me. And they had thrown us together, against one another. So who was I in that moment? Not a hero, avenging my people. Just a poor black man killing other poor black men on behalf of rich white men whose power games brought us to the edges of hell.

Then I did it. I put my rifle to a face not all that different to mine. And it wasn't exciting. It didn't feel like justice. I don't regret it, that war needed winning. But when I killed that miserable man, it felt like I'd murdered my own history for a future I would never, ever be a part of.

Silence.

Jyoti   I'm sorry.

David   Don't be. It's just the way of things. But we won't leave them like that.

A beat. **Jyoti** *digs something out of her bag. A coin. She holds it up.*

What's this?

Jyoti   A quarter rupee. My mother left it to me. For luck. To keep me safe . . . so consider that a promise. On my luck. I won't tell Rasik.

She hands the coin to **David**.

I'll keep you safe.

David   Thank you.

A beat.

Maybe you could join us?

Jyoti   One step at a time, cowboy.

David   Heh.

David *pockets the coin.*

I do love your husband. But he's wrong about a great many things. Justice isn't certain. The future isn't a destination.

It's only where you make it.

6. Nairobi Suburbs, Kenya

Months later. **Rasik** *and* **Jyoti***'s house. Night. A dark bedroom.* **Jyoti** *asleep.*

Rasik *writes a letter by lamp light. He narrates to the audience as he does so.*

Rasik   Dear Shantiben,

On behalf of myself and Jyoti, I am responding to your letter of the 3rd March. Things in Nairobi are fabulous, thank you for asking, we have really found our feet. The violence continues here and there but so far we are unaffected.

Behind him, **Jyoti** *shoots up from bed.* **Rasik** *turns to her.*

Rasik   What's wrong?

Jyoti   I'm ok.

Rasik   It's still dark. You can sleep some more.

Jyoti   Just wanted to get up.

She cries in pain.

Rasik   My God, let me . . .

Jyoti   It's happening, Rasik.

Rasik   Woah.

Jyoti   You understand?

It's happening.

Are you?

You are, you're crying.

You're fucking crying, you're –

Rasik *spins back to the audience, the letter.*

Rasik   I'm sorry to hear that your husband is ill. I'm more sorry that I'm not able to act on your request to help with the children. Jyoti is, naturally, devastated.

Jyoti   TELL HER TO KISS MY HAIRY – !

Rasik   She sends her love.

I've enclosed some money that I hope will help. It is a trying time for us you see, but also an exciting one because the baby is almost due! Jyoti is *very* happy about this, as I'm sure you can imagine.

Jyoti   Motherfucker!

Rasik *is back in the scene with* **Jyoti**.

Rasik   Language. Please Jyoti, there are people . . .

Jyoti   Fuck off. This is –

Rasik   A miracle.

Jyoti   A miracle if you want one, I didn't want one. I'll kill it, I'll kill –

Rasik   Shut up, you don't mean that.

Jyoti   Yeah? Come here and I'll show you what I mean, I'll – AHHH! This isn't the person I was supposed to be, Rasik. This isn't –

AHHH!

More, I want to do more, I want to do so much, this isn't who I'm meant to –

Rasik   Hold my hand. Look, just hold my hand.

She breathes hard.

I'm here. We'll be OK.

Jyoti   I –

AHHH!

Rasik   I'll find someone.

Jyoti   No! No! No no no no no no.

Don't go!

Don't –

The world goes soft. **Rasik**, *eyes wide, narrates a letter again.*

Rasik   You will not believe this, Shantiben, but –

Rasik *holds the baby in his hands.*

Sonal. Her name is Sonal. We've been so blessed.

It is clearly the greatest sight he has seen in his life. He returns to **Jyoti**.

You said something?

Jyoti   I said don't go anywhere. Please.

Rasik   I won't, I'm never leaving you ever again. Not your
. . .

Not our. Not our girl.

Rasik *hands* **Jyoti** *the baby. She looks at it. In a moment, her doubts vanish.*

Jyoti   Our girl.

David   Are you ready?

Jyoti *and* **Rasik** *turn –* **David** *stands waiting with* **Rasik**'s *camera.*

Jyoti, **Rasik** *and daughter pose. It's comfortable. Cute. The perfect moment.*

David *laughs as he hits the shutter. A muffled CRACK accompanies the BLINDING flash.*

Jyoti What?

The muffled crack again. **David** *hands* **Rasik** *the photo, leaves.*

What's that sound?

She strains to look up. Another noise grows in intensity. A crowd?

Rasik, what's that sound?

It gets louder still. **Rasik** *moves to the window.*

Rasik There's –

There's a lot of people outside.

Gunshots echo. **Rasik** *watches, horrified.*

Jyoti David?

Rasik No it's ok, he's not there.

Jyoti But David. He's –

Involved.

A beat.

Rasik I should've said.

Jyoti *looks at her daughter. Hers. Precious. Vulnerable.*

Absolutely, I should've said but he's harmless, he's just . . . a supporter. A well-wisher, he doesn't really do any –

Jyoti Rasik, I have to –

A bright FLASH. **Rasik** *squeezes his eyes closed.*

7. Nairobi City Centre, Kenya

Rasik *opens his eyes. He looks exhausted. We see he's now in a cinema.*

Newsreels playing. Over dramatic music, the flickering screen shows remains of atrocities. Burnt-out villages. Dead bodies. Mau Mau violence.

Rasik*'s eyes droop as a wide shot of a prison appears. An image of captured fighters in a line. Close-up on one of their faces as they turn to the camera. A flicker. The face becomes* **David***'s.*

Rasik *bolts upright. A flicker. The face returns to normal.*

An image of a hotel burning. A sign, licked by flames, with the letters: PALACE HOTEL. **Rasik***, attention piqued, leans forward.*

Newscaster   With a flare up in rebel violence and stricter curfews coming into effect, the House of Commons met last week to discuss the investigation into prisoner mistreatment at the Hola detention camp . . .

Extracts from the House of Commons Debate regarding Hola Concentration Camp – 27th July 1959. The words of the Honourable Member of Wolverhampton South West – one Enoch Powell.

Powell   It is argued that this is Africa, that things are different there. Of course they are. The question whether the difference between things there and here is such that the taking of responsibility there and here should be upon different principles.

Another man enters the cinema. **Rasik** *squints to see him. Can't make him out.*

We cannot say, 'We will have African standards in Africa, Asian standards in Asia and perhaps British standards here at home.' We have not that choice to make. We must be consistent.

The man moves towards the screen. **Powell***'s voice continues . . .*

What we can do in Africa depends upon the opinion which is entertained of the way in which this country acts and the way in which Englishmen act. We cannot, we dare not, in Africa of all places, fall below our own highest standards in the acceptance of responsibility.

Rasik *withdraws as the man ENTERS the cinema screen and now we see him so clearly. It's* **Rasik**. *Older. Smarter suit. Stronger. Bolder. An ideal image.*

Younger **Rasik** *starts to mutter something to himself. Can't quite hear it. A list?*

The newsreel finishes. The man flickers away to black.

God Save The Queen plays. **Rasik** *rises to his feet, stares at the blank screen.*

Darkness falls. As it does, **Rasik** *reaches down, picks up something.*

A lantern.

8. Outskirts of Nairobi, Kenya

The farm. Twilight.

Rasik, *lantern in his hand, steps cautiously through the gloom. Shapes seem to move in the shadows.*

David   Rasik?

Rasik *spins to find* **David**, *sitting in the entrance to the barn.*

A home-made rifle in his lap.

Bit late for a stroll, my friend.

Rasik   A fine night is a fine night . . .

He gestures around.

Who wouldn't want to walk through fields like this?

David   Hard-working men. Modern technology. A productive combination.

Rasik *points to the rifle.*

Rasik   Yes, and I know I'm new to this, David, but I don't think I'm familiar with *that* particular bit of irrigation equipment.

David   Oh. Would you like me to show you how it works?

He stands. **Rasik** *flinches.* **David** *puts the rifle down. Sighs.*

She told you.

He pulls out the coin from his pocket. Looks at it.

Rasik   She was worried. Did you expect her not to?

A beat. **David** *pockets the coin again.*

David   Doesn't matter now anyway.

Rasik   You promised me you wouldn't do this. I said, we can be partners, I bring the money, you bring the men, this can be your home, you do what you need to make your interests work for you, I won't ask questions just don't make it impossible for me to –

David   Oh look at you, Rasik. Years later, still giving me orders outside my own home.

Rasik   It's not an order –

David   The British are trying to crush the last of us. And they're using your people to do it.

Rasik   My people? What about *your* people, they're sick of your actions. You don't speak for all of them.

David   No. But when we win . . . they'll say we did.

Rasik   Deluded.

David   Is this uncomfortable for you? I'm sorry that you're not able to keep a profitable ignorance anymore, but that's not my problem.

A beat.

Rasik   It's still profitable.

David   What?

Rasik   This land is still valuable, David. That's what I've come to tell you. I'm selling it and we're leaving. We can't bring Sonal up here, surely you understand that it wouldn't be –

David And what about my children? What happens to them?

Rasik I don't know. But this can still work out nicely for everyone.

David You're selling my home, how does that 'work out' for me?

Rasik Use the money. Buy somewhere of your own. The law allows it now, things are changing, for the better, just like I said.

David And you expect me to be grateful for that? Buying back what was always mine? No no, I could buy as much land as I like, pay whatever price, but it wouldn't be clean. Not while the whites still have their fingers in this dirt.

Rasik That'll change. But if you keep going like this, you won't live to see it.

David Get out of here.

Rasik I can't give you justice. Only money, and that's not nothing.

David What if I say no?

Rasik No?

David To the sale. What then, partner?

David *stands.* **Rasik** *suddenly aware of the shapes around him.*

Don't worry about my men, they don't see you as a threat.

A beat. **Rasik** *finds his courage.*

Rasik Me telling you is a courtesy, I hope you understand that.

David Ahhh. And there it is. Our partnership.

Rasik *shakes his head. Goes to leave.*

Rasik   I nearly mistook you for a pragmatic man, David.

David   And I nearly mistook you for a Kenyan, Rasik.

9. Nairobi Sururbs, Kenya

Jyoti *and* **Rasik***'s house.*

There are suitcases laid out in front of them. They're packing. It's quiet. Efficient. Unhurried.

Jyoti *tries to shut a suitcase. Can't manage it. She pushes all her weight onto it. Doesn't do it.*

Rasik   Here.

He lifts her onto the suitcase. She sits, squashing it just enough for **Rasik** *to zip it closed.* **Jyoti** *smiles at him.*

Jyoti   The mighty strength of Tarzan!

She takes his hands.

Rasik   You're nervous?

Jyoti   Just I was –

I was starting to see it, you know? Walking Sonal to school. Us all taking the train to Mombasa on the weekend, head out the window, looking for lions.

Rasik   They have lions in London too.

Jyoti   Stone lions.

Rasik *returns to packing his case.*

Rasik   Sure, but at least you can sit on them. Try that on the ones here . . .

A knock at the door. **Jyoti** *looks to* **Rasik**.

Don't answer it.

They go back to packing.

Knocking again. Louder. More insistent. The sound of a baby stirring.

Jyoti   It'll wake her up.

She goes to the door. Opens it.

Rasik   Don't . . . !

Too late. **Jyoti** *stares at the person at the door.* **David***, ragged, breathless.*

What are you doing here?

David   I . . .

Rasik   The nerve of you . . .

Jyoti (*To* **Rasik***.*)   Get him some water.

A beat. **Rasik** *stares at* **David***.*

Rasik! Get him some water.

Rasik *reluctant, but goes to fetch water.* **David** *sits.*

(*To* **David***.*) Are you ok? What happened?

David *spots the suitcases.*

David   Holiday is it?

A beat.

Jyoti   London.

David   The belly of the beast. Where else?

Jyoti   It's not forever.

David   Uhuh.

Rasik *returns with the water.*

Rasik   You look awful.

David   Thank you.

Jyoti   It's gone curfew.

David   Yes, the soldiers who chased me the last five blocks made that clear.

Rasik   You – ! Soldiers!

Jyoti *goes to the window. Checks.*

Rasik   If they find you here they'll –

David   That's not going to happen, they didn't see me come here.

Jyoti   No one there.

She pulls down the blinds, shuts the door. **Rasik** *stares at* **David**.

Rasik   I still have the money. Is that what you want?

He fetches the money.

You can have it. If you just go now.

David   I don't need money, I need a friend. I was trying to make it back, to my heh. Lodgings. It's still there, just about. But one of those Home Guards recognised me, used to serve in the same unit, the traitor and now –

I'll sleep in a coal sack if you want me to.

He sees **Rasik** *is a dead end. He turns to* **Jyoti**.

But let me stay til sunrise. Then you never have to see me again.

Jyoti *turns to* **Rasik**.

Jyoti   Would it be so bad?

Rasik *laughs.*

Rasik   Bad? If they find him here, they'll never let us leave. And do you know what his mob have been up to? They murdered an Asian family. Last weekend. You heard about that?

A pause. **Jyoti** *looks at* **David**, *seeking explanation.*

David   That wasn't me. But it doesn't matter. The military, they're after everyone, it doesn't matter if you're innocent or not.

Rasik   You think you're innocent? Butchering 'traitors', your countrymen. You've killed more of your people than you have white men!

Jyoti   Rasik, stop.

Rasik   He told you the story, right? About Ethiopia? It's a real gripper, that. But did he ever tell you about Lari? Children, women, clubs, knives and fire.

Back to **David**.

Tell me your justice hasn't made life worse for everyone.

David   I can't call myself innocent. I've been a part of events I regret . . .

Rasik   'Events.'

David   . . . but there's no malice to me, Rasik, not to you. Not to Jyoti . . .

Rasik   Not *yet*.

David   . . . I'm as I ever was, looking to make things work for my children, their children, they can't come into a world like this, you can understand something of that.

Jyoti   You were out on a mission?

A beat.

To kill someone?

David   Jyoti . . .

Rasik   The Mau Mau are done, David. There's nothing left to fight for.

David   Then why are you running? Eh? If it's over, what are you scared of?

Is it me? Are you scared that I might win? Because we are going to win.

A pause.

Jyoti   You will. And that does scare me. Your hope scares me because I don't know what lies on the other end of that hope for people like us.

David   Please don't indulge the version of me that's in your head, look at the man in front of you who's –

Jyoti   How many kids have you killed?

A beat.

You like to talk about children so much, you must've kept count, I know I would, I know that's a figure I'd keep an eye on.

Did they deserve it? If it was Wambui's child, would you think that –

David   Wambui's dead. British bombers levelled the forest camps last week. Her boy survived, I pulled him from under a burning tree.

A pained beat.

No one ever deserves it.

Sonal, *in the other room, begins to cry.* **Rasik** *goes to her.*

Jyoti   I think you should go.

David   I don't know if I'll make it back.

A beat.

Jyoti   Skip the fence, take the alleyway behind the house. You'll have a better chance going that way.

David *stands, walks towards* **Jyoti**. *She looks at him with infinite care.*

You're a resourceful man, David. I have faith you'll be fine.

He leaves, slamming the door. **Jyoti** *stares after him.*

Rasik *comes to* **Jyoti**'*s side, holding* **Sonal**.

Jyoti   It was the right thing. The right thing for Sonal.

Rasik   Of course. Don't give it another thought.

Jyoti *keeps staring at the door. Blackout.*

End of Act One.

Two

1968–1977

1. London, England

1968. **Jyoti** *addresses someone we can't see. She's dressed in a sari, with a workman's jacket over the top. In one hand she holds an infant, in the other is a half-eaten sandwich. She's on a bustling picket line.*

She responds, timidly, to questions we cannot hear.

Jyoti   Do I –

Do I reply to you or to the camera?

To you, ok.

Hm?

You're on a what? A wide angle? I don't know what that is.

Right. So I should probably? Yep.

She throws the sandwich aside.

Ok! Ready.

She breaks into a big smile.

Hello! My name is Jyoti Karia!

Oh. Sure, no problem.

She talks again, clearer, more deliberate.

Hello my name is Jyoti Karia. I arrived in London in 1959 and I've been at Bushwood Manufacturing in Willesden for about six years now. I have two beautiful daughters, Sonal who's eight and this here is little Roshni, careful she's quite bitey heh –

Yes, my husband is very supportive of me, cuts meat in the day and sells fruit at night, all the major food groups covered. Although he'd want me to say that he's looking for a traineeship if anyone out there is –

Oh! You meant . . . heh, no. no. I'm not one of the striking women, this isn't my factory, I'm just here to support. Find it so inspiring.

No, um, the management where I am are better than most, I think.

Uh I have had trouble, of course. Some of the men, they would uh spit at me, call me a wog, a Paki, you know?

Huh? Ok. Yes, of course, sorry.

Not at all, I understand, I absolutely don't want to offend your audience with such language. Let me –

She adjusts herself.

I have had trouble. They didn't like me when I first arrived, some of the men . . . I won't go into it . . . but I've proved myself to them. They only thing they call me now is 'boss'.

I'm not – no, I'm not their *actual* boss, but what I've seen the last few weeks, what I've seen women do here in Dagenham, in Halewood, tells me that the world and the workplace can and will be better. I don't like to linger on the past. And women will change this country.

Do I feel it? Absolutely. A friend once told me 'the future is where you make it'.

And just like those cars in there, it's being made here in Britain.

Filming stops. **Jyoti** *relaxes into a smile.*

Cor, that was a cracking end line, wasn't it! Really happy with myself there, don't know where it came from, it just – POP! – and out it –

No, thank *you*, sorry if I got a bit –

Ok thanks, good to know.

Will this – ?

Are you showing this documentary in the cinemas? You see I've always wanted to be on the –

Ah. Television's better anyway. Bigger reach.

A beat.

A small woman on a small screen! Heh.

She smiles.

Suits me.

The world slides on.

2. London, England

Four years later. The living room/kitchen of a small flat. A front door off to one side, bedrooms off on the other. It's afternoon.

Rasik, *scruffy, in a Liverpool shirt, asleep at a makeshift desk with books and paper on it. He snores gently.*

A key in the door. Through the door comes **Jyoti** *with a shopping bag. She sees* **Rasik** *asleep.*

From a bedroom comes **Sonal**, *thirteen years old. She spots* **Jyoti**.

Sonal   Hey Mum.

Jyoti   Shhh!

Jyoti *points at* **Rasik**.

Sonal   What are you doing?

Jyoti (*Whispering.*)   Sonal. Come here.

Sonal (*Now also whispering.*)   Why?

Jyoti   Come here.

Sonal Why though?

Jyoti 'Why why why' Why are you always like this?!

Sonal I'm not always like anything, no one can always be like one thing.

Jyoti Stop being a smart-arse and just come here, will you!

Sonal *comes to* **Jyoti**. **Jyoti** *presses a party horn into her hand, points to* **Rasik**. **Sonal** *smiles – she gets it.*

They move towards him slowly, take up positions either side of him, a pincer formation. **Jyoti** *indicates a countdown – Three, two, one. BOOM!*

Rasik FUCK ME!

Rasik *shoots up, tumbles off his chair.*

Jyoti *and* **Sonal** *fall about laughing.*

What was that?! What's going on?!

Jyoti We're celebrating!

Sonal Are we?

Jyoti Yes.

Sonal Oh. We're celebrating, Dad.

Rasik What? What are we celebrating?

Jyoti You passing your exam.

Rasik *stands up, collects himself.*

Rasik Oh.

That's nothing . . .

He gestures at the books.

There's like fifty of them.

Jyoti Then you're one-fiftieth towards being a surveyor, so we celebrate that.

She pulls a nice cake out of the bag, places it on the desk.

Rasik   Blimey, how much did that cost you?

Sonal   Way to kill the mood, Dad . . .

Jyoti   It's my money to waste.

Rasik   I know but –

Jyoti   And it's personalised, so they're not taking it back now.

Sonal *inspects the cake.*

Sonal   Who's 'Russ'?

Jyoti   Russ is the person who's going to kick you up the bum unless you get me a knife and some matches.

Sonal   Ugh.

Jyoti   Don't 'ugh' me, young lady, get to it.

Sonal *skulks slowly to the kitchen units.*

Sonal   This would never happen on the planet Triacus.

Jyoti   What on the where now?

Sonal   Children are in charge on the planet Triacus.

Jyoti *looks to* **Rasik***: 'Does this make sense to you?'*

Rasik   It's that TV show . . . *Star* . . . *Mates.*

Sonal   *Trek. Star Trek.*

Rasik   She watches at her friend's house.

Sonal   He has a name.

Jyoti   He?

Sonal   Adam.

Jyoti   I don't like the sound of this 'he'.

Sonal *picks up a knife. Much larger than is necessary.*

Sonal   Well if we had a telly I wouldn't need to be friends with Adam, would I?

Jyoti (*Playful.*)   Oh I see! and who's going to pay for that. You?

Sonal *grins, cheeky.*

Sonal   Sure. If you up my pocket money.

Rasik   Up it? You're already getting paid more than I am . . .

I should get changed.

Jyoti   You look fine.

Rasik   You've made an effort, I should make one too . . .

A crack! **Sonal** *stands holding a cupboard door, matter-of-fact.*

Sonal   Door came off again.

Jyoti   Oh for God's sake.

Rasik   I was meant to call the landlord about that . . .

Jyoti   I'll do it in the morning. *You* go get changed, and *you* get me those matches, they're in the other cupboard, top shelf.

Rasik   Back in a sec.

He exits to a bedroom.

Jyoti   Where the fuck is Roshni?

Sonal   She's next door.

Jyoti   Again?

Sonal *returns with the knife and matches.*

Sonal   Yeah, Dad said he thought she kept . . . looking at him.

Jyoti   Right . . .

Sonal   Said it was distracting. But Kamlamasi loves taking care of her so everybody wins.

Jyoti   Well we can't keep palming your sister off on a broody brown women who'd kidnap her if she got the chance. You're going to have to step up.

Sonal   I already got you the matches, didn't I?

Jyoti   Not asking for much, just a little help around the flat, a little help with Roshni. Things are getting a bit messy at work and they need me.

Sonal   You? You specifically?

Jyoti   Yes, if you're starting a union, it helps to have someone who enjoys shouting at people.

Sonal   What's a union?

Jyoti   Well.

The new boss makes women, women like me and you, the new boss makes us work longer than the white people, for less money and in worse conditions. And a union is a group of people getting together to help negotiate and stop things like that happening.

Sonal   But why doesn't the boss just pay everyone the same in the first place?

Jyoti   Why indeed! For once, 'why' is a good question, and you need someone to ask questions like that to the the bosses, but they're far away in their big old offices so you need someone very loud, and once again, that's where your mum comes in.

A beat.

Sonal   You are *very* loud.

Jyoti   Right? So are you going to make me shout at you or are you going to help me and all those other women make things better?

Sonal Ugh. I've already got loads of my own things to do you know.

Jyoti You're thirteen, what things do you have to do?

Sonal You didn't have things to do when you were thirteen?

Jyoti I was basically *married* by the time I was thirteen, you want to do that instead? I'll make it happen, you watch.

Sonal Hah, don't lie.

Jyoti I'm not lying.

Sonal You were never thirteen when you were married. I know the story, Dad's told me a million times, the photos, the drink, him twenty-two and you –

Jyoti Fourteen.

Happy? I was a year off. Fourteen.

A beat.

Sonal Seriously?

Jyoti My dad wanted me out the house, wasn't going to wait. And don't you dare tell *your* dad. He doesn't know.

Sonal That's so . . . wrong. Fourteen.

Sonal, *unexpectedly, hugs her mum.* **Jyoti**, *awkward at first, relaxes into it, feels it deeply, like a hug she's needed her whole life.*

You told me something weird. Shall I tell *you* something weird?

Sonal *begins to rock her mum, playfully.*

Jyoti Mmm I'm ok.

Sonal I'll tell you anyway.

Jyoti How kind.

Sonal   Get this – there's nearly twice as many people alive now than when you were born. Twice as many! Tell me that isn't weird.

Jyoti   Uhuh. Teaching you useful things at that fancy school then, are they?

Sonal   Teaching me that we all should do a lot less fucking . . .

Jyoti *scowls at her. Stops the rocking.*

Jyoti   You know I don't like that language.

Sonal   Uhhh? Who'd you think I picked it up from?

She smiles at **Jyoti**. **Jyoti** *smiles back.*

Jyoti   And –

You're not are you . . . ?

Sonal   Am I what?

Jyoti *prepares herself to say a swearword as if it's for the first time in her life.*

Jyoti   'Fucking.'

Sonal   Oh my God.

She pushes herself out of the hug.

Jyoti   Your Adam friend maybe?

Sonal   Oh my God Mum no we are not having this conversation.

Jyoti   Well I promise I'll never ask you what boys you're doing what with, if you promise to be my sidekick.

Sonal   Sidekick?

Jyoti   Like in the Batman. See, I do know some things but I still need my Robin to join me. Because I can't do anything mighty without her.

Sonal *thinks, relents.*

Sonal   Ugh. Fine.

Jyoti   Thank you.

And stop with that 'ugh' noise, makes your face look like a gremlin.

Rasik *returns, wearing a shirt and tie.*

Rasik   Ladies.

Jyoti   Took your time.

Rasik   Wanted to find a tie that matched the cake.

Sonal   Looking sharp, Dad.

Rasik   Thanks, darling.

Jyoti   Right.

She lights the candle.

Now we're all here, maybe we can actually enjoy ourselves, yeah?

She gestures to the cake. **Rasik** *steps over, carefully holds back his tie, blows out the candle.*

The world slides on.

3. London, England

Two years later. The same flat. Late night.

Jyoti *is painting protest placards.* **Rasik**, *in a shirt and a loosened tie, is half-cut.* **Jyoti** *doesn't look at him.*

Rasik   Evening!

Jyoti   You stink.

Rasik   Stink is unfair . . .

Jyoti   It's exactly fair, you stink of booze . . . and meat?

Rasik   No!

Jyoti   I thought we'd be done with your meat stinks after you left the butchers but here we are again . . .

Rasik   That's not meat, dear. That's . . . love.

On that horrendous note, **Jyoti** *turns to* **Rasik**.

Jyoti   No.

Rasik   Yes.

Jyoti   No.

Rasik   Oh yes.

Jyoti   No, it's . . .

Rasik *steps in, pecks her on the lips.* **Jyoti** *sniffs.*

. . . kebab. Since when do you eat kebabs?

Rasik   I told you, it's not kebabs, it's love.

Jyoti   Love doesn't smell like kebab.

Rasik   And how would you know?

A beat.

Jyoti   Well. Guess you got me there.

Rasik   I talked about you tonight.

Jyoti   Uh oh.

Rasik   No no, it was good, it was a good thing, I was really selling you.

Jyoti   Thanks?

Rasik   Yeah like I told them about the school, how you got Sonal into that great school I told them how you marched straight in there and said 'Look! My family have been subjects of this country since before I even came here, since the day I was born. I paid my respects. I paid my taxes. I cheered us winning the World Cup the other year . . .'

Jyoti   I didn't say *that*.

Rasik   '. . . I cheered even though I hate the bloody football . . .'

Jyoti   I never said that, you're making that up.

Rasik   '. . . so you *will* educate my girl, madame, I have earned her the right to get what I never had!' And now she's thriving! Heh. Their faces. You should've seen.

Jyoti   So you're becoming a real part of the team now, huh?

Rasik   An *invaluable* part of the team.

Jyoti   What does that mean? A promotion soon? Or just more exams?

Rasik   Well you know. Promotions aren't just about the exams, there's groundwork to be laid . . .

Jyoti (*Gently mocking.*)   Groundwork! That's what you call this? Foundations made of doner meat and greasy chips.

Rasik   Yeah I mean. No point in passing exams if they don't respect your social abilities. And half of that is fending off the fuckers.

Like, there's this Owens guy – he wants the big job when Mr Bailey goes, head of the surveying team – so he's been spreading these lies, says I'm sympathetic to the Chinese, that I'm a communist, and I swear he's hired someone to –

Jyoti   Someone to what?

Rasik   All I'm saying is, and it might be nothing, but sometimes it feels like there's a man following me, spying on me. I swear to God, that's the lengths some of them would go to, that's how desperate someone of them are to not see a talent like me succeed.

Jyoti *considers how to handle her paranoid husband.*

Jyoti   That must be difficult, dear.

Rasik *begins to pace the living room.*

Rasik   And he's a bigot too on top of everything else! Owens. You know what he said to me? He came up to me, I was cleaning the cups, in the staff room, and he came up to me and asked 'why do your women wear wallpaper?'. This little swagger on him, this nasty tone 'why do your women wear wallpapers?'

Heh. And you know what I said back to him? You know what I said back to that bastard? I said 'You mark my words, Owens, one day those woman who wear wallpaper will take your job!' Hah.

A beat.

Jyoti   You're still cleaning cups.

Rasik   Sorry?

Jyoti   That's not what you're there to do, is it? You're not a trainee anymore.

Shrugs, tries to laugh it off.

Rasik   A British man's cups should not have stains on them.

Jyoti   Do any of the other British men bother to clean them or is it just you?

Does Owens clean cups?

A beat. **Rasik***'s mood shifts.*

Rasik   I'm aware that it's slow going, I'm aware you think I'll be stuck doing exams for ever –

Jyoti   I haven't said anything like that . . .

Rasik   But I will find a way through this, hm?

A beat. **Rasik***'s high spirits return.*

For now though . . . I'm going to bed!

Jyoti   Probably a good idea.

Rasik   Do you want to come with me?

He steps in close, smiles at her. A beat.

Jyoti   I'm ok.

Rasik   You're 'ok'?

Jyoti   Yeah I can't I've still got –

Rasik   I promise I'll wash my hands and everything.

Jyoti *laughs.*

Jyoti   Oh I'm a lucky woman!

She smiles back at him. Thinks about going . . .

Just. They're relying on me, I've got loads more to do before the morning and I'm already behind, so . . .

A beat. **Rasik** *tries to sweep* **Jyoti** *off her feet but she's not expecting it, thrashes, knocks her materials everywhere.*

Jyoti   Shit!

Rasik *drops her.*

Rasik   You got paint on the carpet.

Jyoti *scoff-laughs, incredulous at being blamed. But knows better than to say anything. She starts to clean up.* **Rasik** *stands for a second, watching.*

He nods, realising the 'moment' has passed, scuffs the carpet with his foot.

Doesn't matter. It's a state anyway . . .

He drifts off to the bedroom. **Jyoti** *watches him go. Returns to her placard.*

The other door opens quietly. **Sonal**, *now fifteen, enters.*

Jyoti   Sorry dear, did we wake you up?

Sonal   Nah. Couldn't sleep anyway.

She nods towards the placards.

Those for the typewriter factory strike?

Jyoti   Uhuh. Want to help?

Jyoti *holds out a paintbrush to* **Sonal**. **Sonal** *takes it, begins to paint.*

Sonal   How are they doing up there?

Jyoti   Four weeks in, no union recognition, but still holding the line. My God you should see it, Sonal! A hundred Asian sisters, howling and hollering at any scab who tried to get past! Fury echoing down the streets. Even the policemen are scared of them!

Sonal   Amazing. I'd *love* to see that.

Jyoti   Leicester doesn't know what's hit it!

Sonal   'Course I *can't* though can I cause I'm stuck looking after my actual sister . . .

Jyoti   I'm very grateful, I've said I'm grateful.

Sonal   Just be nice if Roshni didn't throw a tantrum every time I cooked for her.

Jyoti (*Playful.*)   Good practice for your own kids.

Sonal   I was *never* that bad.

Jyoti   Ahh how quickly we rewrite history.

They return to painting.

Sonal   So you're off to Leicester in the morning, then back for the late shift.

Jyoti   You know it.

Sonal   The paki shift.

Jyoti *stops painting.* **Sonal** *continues.*

That's what Adam says his dad calls the late shift. 'The paki shift.' Which is a bit funny 'cause we're not even from Pakistan, are we?

Jyoti   He said that? When did he say that?

Sonal   Oh. Like. A few months ago? I dunno, it's not a big deal.

Jyoti   You can always talk to me about things like that if they upset you.

Sonal *stops painting, looks at her mum.*

Sonal   Heh.

Jyoti   What, that's funny too?

Sonal   No just I think this is first time I've seen you in like a week.

Jyoti   I know, I'm sorry but I have to –

Sonal   Why don't they just leave?

Jyoti   Who?

Sonal   The women. At the factory. I don't get why they don't just leave, get a job somewhere else, somewhere better.

Jyoti   Even if they could, even if they somehow managed that, they'd just be leaving the problem behind for the next person. That's who all this is really for. The next person. And the next. You understand, right?

Sonal   Yeah. I just get worried about you to be honest.

Jyoti   You're worried about *me*?

Sonal   Bussing all over, pissing off the police, never sleeping.

A beat.

Plus you're ageing horribly. Brown really does let you down.

Jyoti   Oh haha . . .

Sonal *smiles, spins her placard she's painted towards* **Jyoti**, *picks it up. It reads: EQUAL PAY FOR SONAL. She might chant it as a slogan.*

Sonal   Just gonna carry this around the flat I think . . .

Jyoti   Remind me not to ask you for help again.

Sonal   That's the idea.

They share a still, warm moment.

Jyoti   You don't have to worry about me. I know what I'm doing.

Sonal *puts the placard down.*

Sonal   Just promise me you'll get some sleep before morning.

Jyoti *nods,* **Sonal** *leaves.* **Jyoti** *watches her go. She continues painting.*

A figure enters the world. But we can't quite make it out. Before **Jyoti** *spots it . . .*

The world slides on.

4. London, England

Three years later. The flat. Much the same, but now a sofa and a small TV sit in the corner. The TV murmurs away on a programme we can't quite make out.

Rasik *sits in the sofa in front of the TV, but he's staring at his older self who's standing still, suited.*

His older self is watching the TV.

Younger **Rasik** *starts to mutter something to himself again. Definitely a list. We might catch the last few words.*

Rasik   . . . Hema, Kajal, Hitesh, Kirti . . .

Sonal, *eighteen, comes in from her bedroom.*

Sonal   Dad?

Elder **Rasik** *walks off. Younger* **Rasik** *turns to* **Sonal**.

Rasik   Oh! Hey.

A beat. **Sonal** *points to the TV.*

Sonal   Got it working then?

Rasik   Yes! Turns out everyone being on strike is a great time to indulge your hobbies.

Come, sit. Look what's on . . .

She squints at the TV.

Sonal   I've seen this episode before.

Rasik   Not like this you haven't.

He pats the sofa. **Sonal** *slumps next to* **Rasik**, *leans onto his shoulder.*

Sonal   Huh.

Rasik   I know, I didn't realise the uniforms were that colour.

Sonal   Me either.

Rasik   I didn't realise *she* was that colour.

Sonal   What colour did you think she was?

Rasik   Blue maybe? One of the aliens.

Sonal   She's not an alien.

Rasik   Well I know that now!

A beat. **Rasik** *enjoys his own company. But* **Sonal** *is clearly not with it.*

Sonal   Hey Dad. Can I talk to you for a second?

Rasik   Uh oh . . .

He reaches into his pocket. Pulls out a bank note. Hands it to her.

Just say next time.

Sonal Dad, no, that's not –

Rasik Take it.

Sonal We're overdue on the water bill, you're both not working . . .

Rasik The bills will get paid, that's not yours to worry about. Take it.

A beat.

Sonal, the whole point of my life has been to have a moment where I can give my daughter money and not worry about it. So do me a favour.

She hesitates. Then takes the note.

Sonal Thank you.

Rasik, *satisfied, goes back to watching the telly.*

But that's not what I wanted . . . I wanted to know if you'd talked to Mum yet. About the Newcastle offer.

Rasik You told her already didn't you?

Sonal She wasn't happy.

Rasik There's a surprise. See, the way to deal with your mum is to just do what you want, then tell her after, she always comes around.

Sonal I don't want her to come around, I want her to understand.

Rasik Hah good luck . . .

Sonal You're on my side, aren't you?

Rasik I helped you with your application didn't I?

Sonal Cause Mum never really hears what I say, but she'll listen to you.

Rasik Nice that you think so.

Sonal She will, if you talk to her. Properly.

A beat.

So will you?

A beat.

Dad!

Rasik Alright.

Sonal Please Dad, I've got to send the forms before Friday and I can't –

Rasik I've said that I would, and I will! I promise you'll go. Don't worry.

Sonal Cool. Thanks. Sorry.

A beat.

Rasik Does this mean I can have my money back?

Sonal Nah.

A key at the door. **Sonal** *turns to* **Rasik**. *He gestures: 'It'll be fine.'*

Jyoti *enters, flustered, carrying bags, the remains of placards.*
She says nothing as she puts the contents of the bags away.
Sonal *stands.*

Sonal Do you want a hand?

Jyoti *says nothing.*

Mum, do you want a hand?

Jyoti I don't want anything, you do what you want.

Sonal *sighs.*

Sonal You're still mad.

Jyoti No.

Sonal You are though.

Sonal *looks to* **Rasik** *to get involved – he doesn't turn away from the TV. Frustrated, she turns back to her mum to go it alone.*

Sonal   It's nothing personal, you're taking this like it's personal.

A beat.

Jyoti   The university down the road is very good.

Sonal   The course up there is better, way better. And I'll come back on weekends, help out then.

Jyoti   Weekends are no good to me.

Sonal   I'm trying to negotiate, thought you'd appreciate that.

Jyoti   I don't *have* to negotiate with you, dear. Trust me, you'll be so much happier if you stay close by.

Sonal   Please don't do that.

Jyoti   What am I doing?

Sonal   Pretending you're helping me when it's all about making it easier for you to go dancing on some picket line.

Jyoti   'Dancing'? I do that for your future, young lady.

Sonal   Really? How does that work?

Jyoti   Sorry?

Sonal   Like. How does you screaming outside some factory help my future? I'm not going to be working in one, am I?

Jyoti   What, you think you're too good for it?

Sonal   No I didn't –

Rasik   Shouldn't she be?

A beat. **Rasik,** *finally involved. He turns his head to them but remains seated.*

Shouldn't she be aiming higher than a factory. Else what are we even doing in this country? Plenty of factories back in India.

A beat.

Jyoti Are you watching the TV, Rasik, or are you in this discussion because you can't do both.

Rasik Neither.

Rasik *stands.*

I'm getting my tobacco.

Jyoti Yes, very useful, thanks . . .

Sonal, *disappointed to see him go. She sighs, goes to* **Jyoti**, *takes her hands.*

Sonal This isn't fair. You guys moved all over, but you won't even let me go a couple of hundred miles!

A beat.

Jyoti I like having you around. I like you being here. There, happy?

Sonal You've got Dad.

Jyoti That's different.

Sonal Do they still spit on you?

Jyoti What?

Sonal When you first came here, they used to spit on you, right?

A beat.

Cause they still spit on me. In the street. They spit, swear. They tell me to go home and heh I don't know what to tell them when they say that . . .

Jyoti You've never mentioned this.

Sonal   'Cause I'm scared, Mum.

Jyoti   Of what?

Sonal   Of you! I'm scared you'll judge me for not being as strong as you.

Jyoti   I wouldn't, I would never –

Sonal   You left two countries to get here. Most people here never leave their home town. How could you ever expect them to understand us? They hate us. They'll always hate us.

Jyoti   And you think that'll be better *outside* of London?

Sonal   They'll be less of them at least.

Jyoti   Sonal, look at me. Look at me. When you've got a degree, no one will be spitting on you, OK? Nobody will tell you what to do. They won't dare. But stay with me. Please.

She kisses her daughter on the forehead. A beat.

Sonal   Maybe you're right, maybe it's the same everywhere.

Maybe I should just go home, like they tell me to.

Jyoti   You are home.

Sonal   I mean home home. Nairobi. Maybe that's what I'd like.

Jyoti   Oh my, where has *this* come from?

Sonal   I could go back, see the farm.

Jyoti   Ah this is your dad's stories again? He left out the good bits on this one.

Sonal   Meet your old friends . . .

Jyoti   We don't have any friends there, they don't want Asians in Africa, they don't like us in Kenya, they threw us out of Uganda.

Sonal   . . . we could all go! Imagine! We could get woken up every day by the birds, by the heat of the sun on our feet . . . home . . .

Jyoti's *never seen her daughter quite like this. Uncertain how to handle it.*

Jyoti   Sonal, do you know what 'home' really is? It's not a place, it isn't a noun. It's a verb. Home is where you fight to be. And that's hard wherever you go.

So do yourself a favour, drop the fantasies and stop listening to your dad, ok?

Sonal   It's nothing to do with Dad, Dad's hopeless. He's fucked it.

Jyoti   Well maybe it's not about relying on him, hey? What I'm doing, the changes I'm trying to make? They'll spread, they will. They'll spread out of the factories, into the city, across the country. We've got so much support now, it'll become unstoppable! A revolution! It's happening, so please don't be impatient.

Sonal   Revolution? What like at the typewriter factory?

Jyoti   That was difficult . . .

Sonal   You threw yourself at that for three months and for what? They shut it down, fired the lot of them. Revolutions don't happen, Mum. Not here. So don't make me hope for something that's not coming.

I can't bear it.

Sonal *goes to leave via the front door.*

Jyoti   Hey! Where are you going?

Sonal   Dunno. Anywhere. Maybe I won't come back.

Jyoti   Heh.

Sonal   You don't believe me.

Jyoti   I *do* believe you, dear. I believe you'll go one day. It's in your blood.

But it's not today.

Sonal *exits.* **Jyoti***, exhausted, takes a seat.* **Rasik** *comes back in, with a pipe, looks around, confused.*

Rasik   What, is she gone?

Jyoti   Thanks for the back up.

Rasik   When do you ever need back up?

Jyoti   I'm trying to keep us together and you're more interested in blowing money on gadgets.

Rasik   I got that television for a great price, it's an investment.

Jyoti   Hah right.

Rasik   And it's for Sonal more than anything, she'll love it.

Jyoti   Oh you're so concerned about Sonal, but had nothing to say just now?

Rasik   You wouldn't have liked what I wanted to say.

Jyoti   Why? What do you want to say?

A beat.

Rasik   I think she should go. She asked me what I thought and I told her, 'go where your heart tells you and we'll be there for you.'

Jyoti   How poetic. Does it make you feel better? Selling her these mad stories.

Rasik   I'm not selling her anything, it's what she wants.

Jyoti   This Newcastle rubbish didn't come from nowhere. Now she's talking about going to Kenya? It'll be bloody India next week! How can she want what she knows nothing about? That's your doing.

Rasik   I swear Jyoti, sometimes it feels like you don't
want your daughter to dream of anything bigger than
this shithole.

Jyoti   I want her to not think that running away is always
the answer.

Rasik   You think we ran away?

Jyoti   Didn't we?

Rasik   There are people dying to be where we are!

Jyoti   And I wish you'd tell your daughter that. Tell her
how lucky she is.

Rasik   She's lucky to be your servant?

Jyoti   Servant!

Rasik   Don't waste Sonal on that, don't hold her back like
you held me back.

A beat.

Jyoti   Excuse me?

Rasik   I'm just saying –

Jyoti   'Held you back'?

Rasik   I'm just saying.

You haven't made it easy for me. I've been patient, I've been
very patient. Surely you can see, your activities, your
involvement with certain groups has a cost. A reputational
cost for me in my workplace.

Jyoti   Wait are you –

Are you blaming *me* for your being stuck?

Rasik   I'm not stuck. Just the things they say about your lot,
makes things difficult when I try to get a look in. They don't
want troublemakers. The strikes are trouble enough as it is.

Jyoti   No one's confusing you for a troublemaker.

Rasik   Jesus, this is why I didn't say anything, you can't see it.

Jyoti   Sorry, who the hell are you trying to be right now? Who is this man, saying that he's patient with *me*? The same man I waited for for a year? The same man I worked double shifts for so he could study.

Rasik   I didn't ask you to do that!

Jyoti   But if I didn't you'd be nowhere! Wouldn't you? Heh, I mean actually you're nowhere now. Even Sonal can see that. So God knows where you'd be if not for me.

Rasik   Happy maybe? Happy at least.

A beat.

I –

I didn't mean that.

Wait. No.

I did. I think I did mean it actually.

Jyoti   You are such an arsehole sometimes.

Rasik   Sometimes you have to be.

Jyoti   This used to be fun. I used to look forward to seeing you. 'Tarzan', I don't remember the last time I called you that. I don't know what's happened to us.

Rasik   Hah, nothing happened to us.

It happened to you.

Jyoti *stares him down. Talks very slowly . . .*

Jyoti   Fuck. Off. You smug, useless bastard.

Rasik *stands.*

Rasik   I will.

Rasik *heads to the door, turns to deliver a parting shot.*

I will fuck off and find our daughter.

He goes. **Jyoti**, *shattered, sits still.*

She looks at the protest paraphernalia surrounding her. Begins to stand.

Fails to do it. The figure from before reemerges, still in shadow.

With almighty effort, **Jyoti** *hauls herself up.*

The figure retreats.

5. London, England

Jyoti *in a sari and workman's jacket. She shivers as she clutches a tattered placard. It's freezing. Raining hard.*

Rasik *enters, fully suited. A newspaper covering his head from the rain.*

Rasik   You're on your own?

He speaks loudly over the rain.

Jyoti   The others are coming.

Rasik   That doesn't look fun.

Jyoti   It's a hunger strike, it's not meant to be fun!

Rasik   Oh. So I better toss this away then.

He holds up a container.

Jyoti   What's that?

Rasik   Sandwich. Your favourite. Lashings of mustard and mayonnaise.

Jyoti *looks at the container, longingly.*

Jyoti   Get under here, it's dry.

Rasik *joins her, they huddle close together. He hands her the container, points behind her. Speaking normally now.*

Rasik   Do they even know you're out here?

Jyoti   They know. And if they think they can get away with just withdrawing their support (*shouting, to the building behind*) they can think again!

Rasik   You're picketing the union, for your union . . . because they won't let you be a union anymore. Look at you. My little Gandhi!

Jyoti   If you've come here to mock me, go do it with your work pals instead.

Rasik   No I'm sorry, I didn't mean –

I'm sorry.

So is it true? That they've suspended all your memberships?

A beat.

I'm here to listen, I promise.

Jyoti   They said they don't like our tactics.

Rasik   I see.

Jyoti   Too aggressive, 'damaging an already imperilled Labour government' blah blah blah.

Rasik   Guess solidarity only goes so far. Proves it though. That their support isn't worth much. Proves that there's no reason for you to be out here.

She looks at him, suspicious.

Jyoti   You're not here to bring me a sandwich, are you, Rasik?

Rasik   Man can't bring his hungry wife a sandwich?

Jyoti   You've never made me a sandwich in your life.

Come on. Out with it.

A beat.

Rasik   You've done your part. It's someone else's turn to step up.

Jyoti   Like who?

A beat.

Rasik   Like me.

He beams, willing her to guess. **Jyoti** *slowly clocks what's happened.*

Jyoti   A promotion?

Rasik   Not just any promotion. *The* promotion. Head of my own surveying team. Build the reputation, build the contacts then go private sector in a couple of years. Only way from here is up, up, up! Now, I'm going to say a number. Fifteen hundred.

Jyoti   Fifteen hundred what?

Rasik   Pounds. Fifteen hundred pounds. That's what they gave me, a bonus.

A beat.

What's that face for?

Jyoti   Nothing I –

I thought there'd be more time.

Rasik   More time? We've been here nearly twenty years, Jyoti!

Jyoti   I know I know . . .

Rasik   This is your success too. You've earned it.

You know that house? The one on the corner of the park? That you point out every time we go past?

Jyoti   Reminds me of home.

Rasik   Well, we're getting that house. I've put the bonus down as a deposit . . .

Jyoti   You what?

Rasik   . . . and by next month we'll have gotten out of that heap we've been stuck in, that makes us hate each other, to somewhere bigger. Nicer. Warmer! Somewhere the girls can be *proud* to come home to, with their own families some day. You could use those genius hands of yours to build our own little kingdom, leave all this behind and –

Jyoti   You mean leave my job.

Rasik   I said leave all this behind.

Though if you want to talk about the job . . . it's kind of already left you.

A beat as **Rasik** *realises that's too sharp, tries to pivot to the positives.*

But that doesn't matter, you don't need it anymore. Hey, we could even take a holiday. Imagine us, little old us, thirty thousand feet above the sea, going somewhere because we *want* to, not because we *have* to!

Jyoti   How did you get the money?

Rasik   Sorry?

Jyoti   The 'bonus'. They don't just hand those out. What did you do?

Rasik   Well. I proved myself.

A pause.

Jyoti   You broke your strike.

A beat.

You're a scab?! I can't believe –

Rasik   Don't call me that!

It was my chance! I never had a break, you know I never had one and then, there it was, a chance to shove it in the face of all those bastards, Tompkins, Barker, OWENS! Bloody Owens! He thinks nothing of you or me, why should

I have solidarity with him? He doesn't deserve it! They never really had it with us, so when I have a chance to show that I *care,* I care for that company when all they do is sit around and . . .

Rasik *finally acknowledges* **Jyoti**'s *silence.*

Jyoti   I feel like. You're laughing at me. You've come here to laugh at me.

Rasik   No no, I know your ladies are decent people, our people, *they* deserve better, but these guys? Jesus, they –

Please. Please don't look at me like that.

Jyoti   Do you think what I'm doing is a joke?

A beat.

Rasik   Not for *you* . . .

Jyoti   Wow. Ok. Can you . . .

Rasik   Jyoti –

Jyoti   I need you to leave?

Go. Please. Let me think for a second, please let me think for a . . .

Rasik *pulls out an envelope from his jacket pocket.*

What's that?

Rasik   Her acceptance letter.

Jyoti   Sonal? Where?

Rasik   To Newcastle. She's going to Newcastle. I promised her she could go, and it's time I started living up to my promises. And not just to her, anything we want can happen, Sonal has her studies, you can stay at home, help Roshni with school, you're so smart . . .

Jyoti   Rasik –

Rasik   . . . smarter than me –

Jyoti   I don't think that's what I –

Rasik   Hey, hey . . .

Listen. Listen to me.

A desperation in his voice here.

I realised something the other week. I was out having a
drink, buttering up one of the clients, and he said he was
surprised that he still loved his wife after all these years and I
realised that I've never said that to you. That's mad, isn't it?
How we've never said that. I've never made you feel like you
deserve, how your father would've wanted, what your
mother would've wished for, I've not delivered *you* what I
promised either but . . .

I love you, Jyoti.

You're my guide, my hero, my north star, you –

Jyoti   Stop.

Please. Stop. Stop giving me the sell, I'm too tired for
the sell.

You don't need to butter me up. I get the idea. I get what
you want.

*They stare at each other. Neither of them quite sure what they're
feeling.*

Rasik   This could be our lives just beginning, if you'll let it.

So will you let it?

Jyoti *looks at the container. Back up to* **Rasik**.

6. London, England

The flat. Mostly packed up. Only the TV and a VHS player remain.
Jyoti *surrounded by boxes, going through them.* **Rasik** *enters.*

Rasik   We're off then.

Jyoti   Ok.

Rasik   You alright?

Jyoti   Uhuh.

Rasik *searching for something.*

Rasik   Have you seen my . . . .

Jyoti   Here.

She throws him his keys.

Rasik   Heh, I swear, I'd lose my own head if it weren't attached!

She smiles at him. Polite more than anything.

Right, back before you know it.

Jyoti   Safe trip.

He nods, goes to the door. Stops. Turns back to her.

Rasik   Hey.

A beat.

You look nice today.

What you've done with your hair. It's nice.

A pause.

Jyoti   Thank you.

A beat.

Rasik   See you in a bit.

He leaves with a spring in his step. **Jyoti** *left alone.*

Sonal, *eighteen, enters, carrying a full backpack. She moves light on her feet, excited. We've never seen her so happy.*

Sonal   Heya!

Jyoti   Hi.

Sonal   Where's Dad?

Jyoti   Gone to the car already.

Sonal *looks around.*

Sonal   I didn't realise we had so much stuff.

Jyoti   Heh. Yeah. If I'm lucky, I'll be done unpacking in the new place before you graduate.

Jyoti *stands. The two women look at each other.*

You have everything?

Sonal   Yeah. Think so!

Jyoti   Said bye to Roshni?

Sonal   Obviously.

Jyoti   Obviously.

A pause.

Come back whenever you feel like.

Sonal   Mum . . .

Jyoti   You'll always have a place with us.

Sonal   I'm going to the North-East mum, not the Moon.

Jyoti   I know.

Sonal   I won't be gone forever.

Jyoti   People always say that. They never mean it.

A glimmer of an old memory in **Jyoti**'s *mind.*

But if you need us, we're here.

Sonal *hugs her mum.*

Sonal   Oh!

Sonal *swings her backpack around, rummages for something. A VHS tape. She hands it to* **Jyoti**.

Wasn't easy to find. Got it from Adam's brother, he works for the station, think he wanted to prove that fascism wasn't genetic.

Jyoti What is it?

Sonal You'll see.

She gives **Jyoti** *a kiss on the cheek.*

I'll ring when I get there.

She leaves. **Jyoti** *looks at the tape in her hand, turns it over. Then looks up and around her. This flat. Their own little world. Giving way to a new one.*

She goes over to the VHS player. Fiddles with it as she figures out how to work it, pushes the tape in, steps back to watch it. The TV flickers to life –

Jyoti (*On the tape.*) Hello my name is Jyoti Karia.

It's the recording of her interview. **Jyoti** *watches it, smiles in recognition.*

I arrived in London in 1959 and uh –

The tape's a bad copy, it skips repeatedly . . .

– I have two beautiful daughters, Sonal who's eight and this here is little Roshni, careful she's –

– not one of the striking women, this isn't my factory, I'm just here to –

– proved myself to them. They only thing they call me now is 'boss'.

Jyoti's *smile fades as the figure reappears. Emerges fully. It's a woman. Her. Older. She wears the same clothes as her younger self.*

– I don't like to linger on the past. And women will change this country.

Younger **Jyoti** *goes. Older* **Jyoti** *fixates on the screen. The tape keeps running.*

Jyoti Do I feel it? Absolutely. A friend once told me 'the future is where you make it'.

And just like those cars in there, it's being made here in Britain.

Blackout.

End of Act Two.

Three

1. Outskirts of Ahmedabad, India

A funeral pyre, blazing sharp and hot.

Jyoti, *now late seventies, wearing expensive clothes and jewellery, stares at the flames. A quiet dignity to her – the confidence of a lifestyle embraced.*

The fire flares and burns out, leaving us in darkness.

Light returns to the world. We are now in a beautiful garden outside **Jyoti**'s *family house. A large tree dominates the space.*

Rasik, *mid-eighties, is sat in wheelchair, inside the house but visible. A catheter runs from under his shirt to a bag attached to his side. He appears to be sleeping.* **Jyoti,** *sits on a bench, stares up into branches of the tree.*

Joy, *thirty, enters. She wears dirty overalls, her face is covered in grime. She looks just like* **Sonal.**

Joy   She planted that the day you left.

Jyoti   Ah! You're back.

Joy   She told me she planted that tree the day you left for Nairobi.

Jyoti   Nairobi! That feels a hundred years ago . . .

Joy   'That's why it's so tall!

Jyoti   Heh.

Joy *starts to tear up a little bit.*

Jyoti, *instinctively, reaches into her bag for a tissue, holds it out for* **Joy. Joy** *lets it hang.*

Joy   A whole funeral without crying, that's strength! Me? I cry at bloody everything! Heh.

Finally, she takes the tissue.

Are you off soon?

Jyoti   We leave in a few hours.

Joy   Aha.

It's a shame you couldn't visit before she died, she could've shown you herself, the garden. She'd been ill a long time.

Jyoti   I know but I hadn't expected her to –

Joy   Direct flights from London every day now.

Jyoti   Yes but she was *always* ill.

A sickening beat.

What I mean is. If I'd known her condition would change so quickly . . .

Joy   Of course, Auntie, of course. Don't worry, it's all done now.

*She hands **Jyoti** back her tissue.*

Excuse me, one moment . . .

Joy *goes into the house.* **Jyoti**, *a little unsettled, returns to looking at the tree.*

Jyoti   Was it big?

Joy (*Off.*)   Hm?

Jyoti   The emergency. Was it a big fire?

Joy *returns with a towel, drying her now wet face and hair.*

Joy   Biggest we've had in years.

Jyoti   Busy work, saving lives.

. . . *Did* you save . . .?

A beat of reluctance to answer.

Sorry, I shouldn't have . . .

Joy Three women on the top floor of a textile factory. And a child.

Jyoti Amazing. So daring!

Joy Daring! Heh. You know, Auntie, Ba would say in that way, I reminded her of you.

Jyoti Really?

Joy Oh yes, she'd say they were right to name me after you because I was just like her oh so brave younger sister, the example to be copied, the bar to be cleared. Heh. Ba *always* talked so much about you, especially in those last weeks. On and on and on . . . she wouldn't stop . . . God . . .

I just wish you'd have called her, even Sonalmasi called her.

Jyoti Did she? Was she well?

Joy You don't talk to your own daughter?

Jyoti She's just so busy over there . . .

Joy Sounds so strange now! A real American.

Jyoti When you're there that long, I guess you just pick up –

Joy Some of the children here, the rich ones, they go to these American schools, they want to sound American. But soon, it'll be the other way around. All the American kids will want to come here, they'll want to have Indian accents. Because India is the future.

Jyoti So I've heard . . .

Joy You know, they used to say Ahmedabad was 'The Manchester of the East', Indians were the faithful 'British of the East', everything we were something of 'the East'.

Joy *starts to pace around* **Jyoti**, *circles her like a shark.*

Then slowly, so slowly, the West sent us their jobs, their companies, their problems to be solved and in return . . .

I guess we sent them you.

And now we're Manchester. You know? Just Manchester. No need for hand-outs, no need for charity.

A beat.

We were *your* charity once, weren't we?

Jyoti   Sorry?

Joy   That's how we knew you'd arrived, when you still used to visit, we'd get home from school and there would be old clothes bursting out of your overfilled suitcase. We had a nickname for you, me and my brothers, embarrassing to say it now but . . . we called you the rag lady. 'The rag lady's come with her riches!'

Oh don't look offended, Auntie, what wonders you brought us! HARD ROCK CAFE PARIS, I HEART NEW YORK, UNIVERSITY OF NEWCASTLE, SEAWORLD 1992, that was my favourite, I still do my cleaning in it.

Jyoti   I thought they'd be useful.

Joy   You felt you were doing us a favour.

Jyoti   It's the same.

Joy   It isn't. Because it didn't cost you a thing.

Whereas Ba, she knew, family must take its strength from the community, no matter the cost. Had she any wealth to pass to us? No! She'd already given it all to the orphanage, to buy computers for the girls, get them the education she never had. That's what a great woman looks like. So I hope you're as proud of her as she was of you.

Jyoti *really wasn't expecting to hear that.*

Jyoti   She never told me she was proud.

Joy   I think perhaps she maybe found you . . . intimidating. But she shouldn't have.

She should never have had to feel like that, because there's nothing about you to fear, and I wish she knew that. I wish she'd have let that tree shrivel. I wish I could tear your name from my soul and replace it with hers, because she gave up so much and you –

Jyoti   You think I didn't?!

Jyoti *stands, with some difficulty.*

Jyoti   You think I don't know that it costs so much more to give something up than to get it? No one ever tells you. But I know.

A beat.

Joy   I've upset you.

Jyoti   You've insulted me. I understand you're sad, I understand that you're angry, but don't you dare tell me that I don't know that.

Joy, *chastened, looks down.*

Joy   I'm sorry, Auntie, I'm just . . .

Jyoti *tilts* **Joy**'s *chin back up. Holds her cheek, tenderly. A matriarch in action.*

Jyoti   It's alright, dear.

Do you need help before we go? I can make dinner.

A truce. **Joy** *shakes her head. She takes* **Jyoti**'s *hands.*

Joy   You're still our guests, Auntie. Rest.

Joy *leaves. Stillness as we see the conversation hit* **Jyoti**. *She looks up at the tree, might begin to cry. She takes a second to pull herself together.*

She goes over to **Rasik**, *slumped in the wheelchair.*

Jyoti   Hope you're having more fun than me.

Nothing from **Rasik**.

She pokes him.

Hey!

Still nothing. Worry starts to overcome **Jyoti**.

Rasik?

Suddenly, he springs his torso up, wide awake.

Rasik   Boo!

Rasik *is super pleased with himself. But* **Jyoti** *is unmoved and unsurprised.*

Oh I was so sure I'd get you this time.

Jyoti   You don't think that's inappropriate? Playing dead right now?

Rasik   I think . . . it's what she would've wanted.

Jyoti   Uhuh.

Rasik   The phone rang by the way.

Jyoti   You can't answer the phone now?

Jyoti *digs the phone out from* **Rasik**'s *pocket.*

Rasik   Touchscreen, I can't work the touchscreen, I told you not to get it. My poor old fingers . . .

Jyoti   Uhuh.

Rasik (*In a creepy voice.*)   Buttons . . . we need buttons . . . heh.

Rasik *laughs at his own performance. Coughs, hard.* **Jyoti** *checks his fingers.*

Jyoti   God, these *are* pretty shrivelled. I'm getting you on the moisturiser.

The phone buzzes. A call incoming. **Jyoti** *answers it, walks away from* **Rasik.**

Roshni   Mum?

It's **Roshni.** *Late forties, on a video call.*

Can you see me?

Jyoti   Sonal?

A beat.

Roshni   No, Mum, it's me it's . . .

Are you ok?

Jyoti   Roshni! Hello!

Roshni   Hey. How'd it go?

A beat.

Jyoti   It was everything she deserved.

Roshni   Aw I'm glad.

Jyoti   How are you?

Roshni   Yeah. Alright.

A beat. Hesitant to say in this context . . .

Bit of a hangover. Kids screaming. *Saturday Kitchen* on the telly. You know, taking it easy and . . . you're doing your face.

Jyoti   What face?

Roshni   Your judgy face.

Jyoti   I don't have a judgy face.

Roshni   Yes you do, Mum, it's instinct, you can't help judging, and it's literally become one of your faces.

Jyoti   That's my thinking face.

Roshni   And what are you thinking about?

Jyoti   You. Your sister.

Roshni   Uh oh . . .

Jyoti   You're happy. Aren't you?

Roshni   Mmm ask me again when half term is over.

Jyoti   Heh . . .

Roshni   We're alright, mum. You just let me know if you need anything.

Jyoti *looks up at the tree.*

Jyoti   I do need something actually.

I need you to rebook our flights.

Roshni   You want to come back later?

Jyoti   No.

We want to come back via Nairobi.

Roshni   Nairobi?! Why?

Jyoti   It's your father's idea.

Roshni   Really? That doesn't sound like something he'd want to –

Jyoti   He's saying, you know, how this might be his last time abroad . . .

Roshni   Yeah but Mum in his condition it's a lot of hassle for him to even –

Jyoti   . . . so he wants to make the most of it, he wants to go to Nairobi.

No. That's not true.

It's me. I want to go.

Roshni   Oh.

Jyoti   I want to see it again. I'll look after your dad, don't worry.

But I'd like to do something for me.

Roshni *takes in what this means.*

Roshni   Huh.

Well, fuck it, good on you, Mum! You deserve a detour. I'll sort it out.

Jyoti   Thank you, dear.

Roshni   Though the kids'll be sad not to see you tomorrow . . .

Jyoti (*Playful.*)   You want someone else for them to scream at you mean?

Roshni   Hey they don't scream at you, they actually *like* you . . .

Rasik   Is that my darling I hear?

Jyoti   Got to go. I love you, dear.

She hangs up.

Rasik   Was that Roshni?

Jyoti   Yes. She wanted to tell us that the flights have been redirected.

Rasik   Ugh. Bloody Air India, they always do this. They always want to keep me trapped in this bastard country . . .

Jyoti   Yeah.

Rasik   Air India. I'm telling you, Jyoti, that used to be a good airline, they've really lost their way, I won't miss them . . .

Jyoti   It's ok. They've got a nice surprise for us actually.

Rasik   Surprise! Ooh, I love a surprise!

Jyoti *smiles. Ready for an adventure.*

2. Nairobi City Centre, Kenya

A bar in the Central Business District. American country music playing.

Rasik *and* **Jyoti** *waiting at a table that's studded with coins.*

Rasik *is in his wheelchair, a duty-free bag on his lap. He doesn't look happy at this surprise.* **Jyoti**, *conversely, really does.*

Rasik   Your toes.

Jyoti   What about them?

Rasik   Look at your toes. You're tapping your toes.

Jyoti   Am I?

Rasik   You are! You're practically . . . *giddy.*

Jyoti   Well. It's a nice song.

Rasik   I don't remember the last time you were giddy. Should I be worried?

Jyoti   No, but you could try to enjoy yourself, Rasik, that's never usually an issue for you.

Rasik   Oh forgive me if I'm not thrilled to be here . . .

Jyoti *catches a scent of something. She sniffs.*

What?

She realises . . .

Jyoti   Have you . . . Oh God's . . .

Jyoti *goes to check* **Rasik** *trousers.*

Rasik   Hey!

She realises – checks his urine drainage bag. Smells it, recoils.

Jyoti   Ugh, you're infected!

Rasik   No I'm not.

Jyoti   That bloody urinary tract infection, it's back again!

Rasik   Leave it, I'm fine!

He bats her away. He thinks.

Though. Maybe we should get it checked out? Yeah, maybe I need to go to the hospital, right now in fact!

Jyoti   Stop it, I know exactly what you're doing.

Rasik   What am I doing?

Jyoti   You're trying to get out of this.

She nods to the wheelchair.

If it pains you to be here, you should've learned to use that thing properly . . .

Rasik   I told you, it's not a thing, he's called Steve.

He pats Steve the wheelchair affectionately.

Jyoti   Well you me and Steve can go to the hospital *after* we're done.

She spots something about the table in front of them.

Rasik   Can you even be sure this is his place? The driver might have been wrong.

Jyoti   It's here.

Rasik   Lots of bars on this road, lots of Davids in general, I don't see him in here and hey we gave it a punt but now we should head back to the airport and –

Jyoti   A quarter rupee.

A hope rises in her.

Rasik   What?

Jyoti   There's a quarter rupee. One of the coins stuck into this table.

Rasik   So?

Jyoti   Never mind . . .

A beat. **Rasik**, *curious, picks up his bag. Sniffs it. At the moment,* **David** *enters. There's a real youthfulness to him. He may well look exactly the same.*

David   If you want a drink, I can do you better than that.

Jyoti   David?

David *doesn't recognise her at first. But a look at* **Rasik**, *then back to a beaming* **Jyoti** *and it clicks . . .*

David   I don't believe it!

Jyoti *on the verge of joyful tears.*

Jyoti   Look at that face!

David *moves with the energy of a man a third of his age.*

David   Look at yours! What are you . . .

Jyoti *rushes to embrace him.*

Woah! Heh. Hello, Jyoti.

Rasik *feels awkward. Left out.*

Rasik   . . . Hello.

David *peels away. He takes in* **Rasik** *fully, briefly shocked by his condition. But hides it well.*

David   Rasik.

How are you doing?

Rasik   Top. Notch.

He makes an 'ok' with his fingers. **David** *clocks a smell, doesn't comment.*

David   Good to see Tarzan's still holding up. That's what she called you right? Tarzan?

Rasik   You told him that?!

Jyoti   I think it's safe to say the King of the Jungle has long since abdicated.

David *shakes his head, smiling.*

David   Ignore her – what can I get you? A Tusker maybe?
Or a pizza?

Rasik   Pizza?

David   Yes, those are our two best sellers.

Jyoti   Don't worry about us. We brought something for *you*
in fact.

She nods to **Rasik**. **Rasik** *pulls a bottle out of his bag.*

David   Wine? Ah . . .

Rasik   Not to your tastes?

David   I don't drink wine, don't know it at all.

Jyoti   You'll like this one.

She hands the bottle to **David**.

Rasik   Duty free, top shelf.

David   1963.

Jyoti   We were lucky to find it! No better year, freedom
for Kenya!

David *stares at her, suspicious.*

Rasik   Do you have any glasses?

David *breaks out of his stare. Finds his smile again.*

David   Hold on.

He goes to the bar, ducks behind it. **Rasik** *turns to* **Jyoti**. *Shrugs.*

Jyoti   Told you it would be ok.

He returns with glasses. **Jyoti** *pours wine into them.*

David   Sure you don't want a pizza? It's not just any old
thing, it's China's favourite!

Jyoti   China?

David   Yes, it's very popular with our Chinese clientele, lots of them here these days, rebuilding that railroad you lot left behind.

Rasik   Hah! Chinese clientele, pizzas and a bar. I would not have guessed.

David   What were you expecting? A farmer maybe?

That comment sucks some warmth from the room. **Jyoti** *doesn't notice.*

Jyoti   Nothing would've surprised me, David.

Jyoti *raises her glass.*

To . . . Kenya's freedom.

Rasik *raises her glasses.* **David** *does not.*

David   Mmm, we should probably toast to something we *all* believe in.

An ugly beat. **Jyoti** *scrabbles for an alternative.*

Jyoti   To you then. To *your* future. To your bar!

David   Heh, what *is* that smile, Jyoti?

Jyoti   I knew I was right to have faith.

David   Faith in what?

Jyoti   That you'd be fine. More than fine. That you'd thrive!

David   I see.

Jyoti   I mean, look at this place! I love the name. 'The Gunmakers'.

David   Named it for the fellow I bought the place from. A fine man, gone too soon.

Rasik   It's a fine location too. Delamere Avenue. David Wachira, finally at the centre of town.

David   Kenyatta Avenue.

Rasik Sorry?

David They changed it. To Kenyatta Avenue.

Rasik Shame! I liked how that came off the tongue. 'Delamere Avenue.'

David Yes, the government in their wisdom decided it would be better to name the main road after the first elected president rather than a white supremacist. Political correctness, what can you do, eh?

Rasik Hah! On the subject of names, you'll like this . . . that colonial secretary . . . you remember?

David . . . Mr Oliver . . . ?

Rasik Mr Oliver Lyttleton. You'll never guess what they named after *him!*

Jyoti A theatre.

David A theatre! Is it nice?

Jyoti Don't know, never been.

Jyoti *pours some more of the wine into glasses.*

But we don't need anything named after us, do we? Only people whose actions can't speak for themselves need that.

She tries to catch his eye as she hands him a glass. He won't turn to her.

David Hm.

And what about Sonal? I bet she grew up the spit of her mother.

Jyoti She's fine.

Rasik She makes films. American films. Science fiction films!

David Really!

Jyoti She *works on* films, as an accountant.

David   You must be proud! I'm very jealous, got no children to feel proud of.

Jyoti   Hard to believe a man like you didn't find a woman.

David   Oh I have family!

He points to the speakers.

This is my nephew playing. Not my real nephew, he's uh – Wambui? You remember. Her son's son. Tells me that country music is the big thing now! He's even teaching me the guitar! Finding my arty side in old age!

He grins.

This is strange, isn't it.

Jyoti   Heh, it is a little.

David   It's strange that you're here. In Nairobi.

Rasik   We're . . .

He looks at **Jyoti**.

Passing through.

Jyoti   Yes, and I thought. Well, you never know do you? At this age. When might be the last chance to catch up with old friends.

David   'Old friends.'

Jyoti   I wanted to see you before it's too late.

David   And so you've seen me. Now what?

A little more warmth vanishes.

Jyoti   . . . I don't know.

David   Uhuh.

David *reaches for the wine, takes a swig. Wrinkles his nose.*

This is good? This is what good wine tastes like? Don't think it suits me.

He empties the bottle onto the floor. **Rasik** *is aghast.*

Jyoti   This was a mistake, a stupid impulsive . . . we'll leave.

She stands.

David   Huh! I thought it was other people you asked to leave, Jyoti!

Rasik   Hey!

Everyone surprised by **Rasik**'s *sudden animation,* **Jyoti** *most of all.*

You don't talk to her like that! She's trying to be nice.

David   Nice?

Jyoti   Rasik, it's fine –

Rasik   I knew it! I knew he would be like this, sour, that's the sort of man he always was!

Jyoti   I don't need you to –

David   You don't know what sort of man I am.

Rasik   Course I do, I had your number since the moment I met you . . .

David   Hah!

Rasik   Wild imagination, no patience, always blaming someone else for his own – !

David   Well you stink, Rasik!

You pathetic wretch. You stink of death, Rasik! Do you know that?

This hits **Rasik** *like a train. The air goes from the room. Eventually, slowly . . .*

Jyoti   But you kept it.

David   What?

Jyoti   The coin.

She taps the table.

You kept it.

David   And you think that means what?

Jyoti   That we could talk? That you would listen. That I could tell you that I tried to make things better, just like you.

Rasik   Don't justify yourself for his sake, Jyoti.

Jyoti   It's not for him.

Rasik   His life's worked out and still he's complaining, always complaining!

The barest hint of a smile moves across **David***'s lips. It's not reassuring.*

David   Worked out. Heh. Let me tell you a story.

David *walks towards the bar as he speaks.*

I took your advice, Jyoti. I took that alleyway, and ran straight into three soldiers out on a patrol. They couldn't believe their luck, I'd fallen straight into their lap! Said they were going to take me to a camp. And I'd heard the stories, it wasn't a place I wanted to go. Shoot me, I said, I'd rather you'd shoot me.

He pulls a knife out from behind the bar, walks back towards **Rasik** *and* **Jyoti.**

After a few days there, with nothing to eat, they dragged me to this big pit, a charcoal pit and they held me over it til the skin on the back crackled like a roast. I still remember being surprised, between my screams, I was surprised at how good I smelled, maybe because I was so hungry and then . . .

He takes in a big breath, slides the knife into the wood of the table, carefully begins to pry out the quarter rupee coin.

. . . they pulled down my trousers and took a bottle, a glass bottle, you know I think it was a Tusker bottle and they pushed it up inside me until it broke and right then I'd had enough, couldn't feel enough to scream anymore which perhaps was encouraging to them because you see that's when they took these pliers, very big, a foot long, they dipped these pliers in that same pit and then what they did, Rasik, is they used those pliers to cut off my left ball first.

All very matter of fact. **Jyoti** *looks away.* **Rasik** *keeps staring.*

Then when the pain faded just a little, they ripped off the right one.

Before I ever really got to use them! Such a shame!

David *laughs, plucks the coin out from the table. He looks to* **Jyoti**.

You didn't come here to find me. I recognise that longing in your eyes. I see it whenever I look in the mirror and ask myself what my life would've been if I hadn't taken that alleyway, if I hadn't trusted you.

He presses the coin into **Jyoti**'s *hands.*

You came here to find yourself, I think. But wherever it is you are, it's not here.

Rasik   I'm –

I never meant for that to happen. We never imagined that you'd –

David   I'm not interested in what you imagined.

A beat. **Jyoti**, *at last, looks at* **David**.

Though there *is* a part of me that's happy to see you, that's happy for your success. Isn't that the strangest thing of all?

A sad smile on his face – warmth from a place of wisdom. He raises a glass.

David   To satisfaction. To more.

To the proud.

To the gone.

3. London, England

Days later. The sound of waves. It's warm. Getting dark.

Jyoti *and* **Rasik** *by a boating lake.* **Jyoti** *wears her old sunglasses, plays with the coin in her hand.* **Rasik** *stares at the water.*

Jyoti   You know, Rasik, I don't think I remember what my dreams were.

But I'm pretty sure Danson Park Watersports Centre wasn't in them.

Rasik   I like it here. Clear water, nice ducks. I like it a lot.

Jyoti   Of course you do.

You said you imagined us on a beach one day. Looking back. Do you remember that? Back in Dandi, just after we got married.

Rasik   No.

Jyoti   Danson Park Watersports Centre isn't the beach that's all I'm saying. Suppose it's for the best. Cruel to look to the horizon at our age.

Rasik *reaches for his drainage bag with an anxious hand, looks at it like it's Yorick's skull.*

I'm going to die soon, aren't I?

Jyoti   Wouldn't make any long-term plans.

Rasik   I don't want to die, Jyoti. Feels like I've only just got started.

Jyoti   It always will.

She pushes up her sunglasses with her free hand.

If *I* die first, and you get worse, who's going to wipe your arse when you go to the toilet?

Rasik *thinks.*

Rasik   Roshni?

Jyoti   Good luck with that, she's got enough on her plate.

Rasik   This is a terrible question to not have an answer for.

Jyoti   And yet it's the most pressing question of your future and mine soon. After all of this, the real biggie. Just who will be left wiping the arses?

Maybe I should just roll you into the lake.

A beat.

Rasik   You said something?

Jyoti   The ground is flat enough, hard enough, I think if I push, you'd roll into the water with quite some speed. Get it over and done with.

Rasik   Are you feeling alright?

Jyoti   What I'm feeling, Rasik, is that I've failed. I have a very precise feeling that I've failed. Don't you feel that too? That our lives were a failure?

Rasik   How can you say that? We've done everything we wanted.

She laughs softly.

Jyoti   No, we've done everything *you* wanted. I got trapped in your story and you built your life on top of mine.

And now I'm just a bitter old woman, a bitter old woman that resents you in a way, an overwhelming way that I can't quite put my finger on and that wasn't what was meant to happen, the old I can live with but I never wanted to be bitter. And the worst thing is that I could've stopped it sooner and I didn't because I thought I loved you in enough little ways except for the right one, the big one.

Rasik   You don't love me anymore?

Jyoti   'Anymore?' You know, right?

You know you've never asked me if I loved you in the first place?

Rasik   I have.

Jyoti   No, you've always told me you loved me, and then –

Rasik   I assumed! That's fair isn't it? That your wife loves you. You've just realised this now?

Jyoti   Just accepted it. I'm sure I always knew. Nothing surprises me anymore.

A beat.

Rasik   I can surprise you.

Jyoti   Yeah?

Rasik   Yeah.

He holds his hands out, about to reveal a great secret.

I was actually twenty-three when I met you, not twenty-two.

He seems very satisfied with that. **Jyoti** *is unimpressed.*

Jyoti   I was fourteen.

A beat.

Rasik   What?

Jyoti   I was fourteen when I met you, not sixteen. So I win, right?

Something stirs in **Rasik**, *like bathtub whisky.*

Rasik   I –

If I'd known, I wouldn't have –

Jyoti   Shouldn't wouldn't couldn't, doesn't matter, too late for that now. What a fucking mess!

She tosses her coin into the water.

What do you think you wanted from your life, Rasik? Before us, before you had to make that pitch.

Rasik   I'm not sure. To be loved? To be needed?

Jyoti   All the fuzzy things.

Rasik   I suppose.

I wanted . . .

For a journey.

For company.

A crack in him.

I wanted my brothers and sisters not to have died before I had a chance to find out who they might've been.

I wanted Sagar.

Deepa.

Vishal.

Priti.

Minal.

Hema.

Kajal.

Hitesh.

Kirti.

Sonal. Roshni. You. I wanted to do right by you all.

He looks to **Jyoti**, *seeking reassurance*. **Jyoti** *doesn't give him it.*

Jyoti   I wanted . . .

I *think* I wanted . . .

A choice.

Rasik   A choice?

Jyoti   A real choice. We're only here because you were what was presented. I thought you were a joke, but a slightly better joke than the others.

And I thought I could handle that. I thought I was going to take whatever I was given and use it to bend the world towards me. But every decision I thought I was free to make since then has hurt someone, so what kind of choices were those anyway? They weren't worth it.

Jyoti *deeply miserable now. The crack in* **Rasik** *widens. He senses his mission.*

Rasik   Would it help if I said sorry?

Jyoti   What are you sorry for? Do you even know why you're saying that?

Rasik   I'm sorry that . . . I'm sorry that you didn't have a choice. But you've done great things. Made a wonderful home, a place for us to feel safe, raised two happy kids . . .

Jyoti   Don't think they're happy.

Rasik   Well even if they're not! All a parent can do is prepare their children for life. And you did. How they live in it, is up to them.

She shakes her head.

Jyoti   Everything I've ever made is soft. I was meant to do better than *soft!*

Rasik   Jyoti, to create softness in a hard world . . . that means something. And I didn't appreciate what it took for you to do that. But I see you now. Cataracts be damned, I see you clearer than I've ever seen you.

Something in this gets to **Jyoti**. *But not all of it.*

You don't believe me.

Rasik *takes a breath.*

Put me in the water.

Jyoti   What?

Rasik   Roll me in like you wanted to, I want to be in.
All the way.

Jyoti   You'll drown.

Rasik   Not true, I can swim.

Jyoti   No you can't.

Rasik   I had lessons.

Jyoti   *When* did you have lessons?

Rasik   I didn't say but I did.

I could teach you even.

Jyoti   Your legs don't work, Rasik.

Rasik   But my arms are still strong!

Ok. Maybe I can swim, maybe I can't. But maybe *this* is what
I'd always wanted. The only adventure left. To give you a
choice. To see you, to see the look on your face as you watch
me on the point of nothing and decide if it's a life you'd
really want. And if it's not, I'll go Jyoti, I promise. Me and
Steve, we'll hit the road, and I'll be ok because I expect
nothing more from the future and stand proud enough of
the past. I know that when I ask myself, when I really ask
myself, what my whole life was about, it wasn't money or
excitement, it all comes down to forever bringing myself
towards you.

That's not what I expected, not what I planned, and maybe
somewhere I got lost, maybe I didn't do as much as I
could've but there's so little I would take back. You're still
the person I wanted to be better for and I want you to know
if you feel that too, you deserve that.

So take me in. Please. Help me give you this choice.

He pops his collar, holds his tie out to her. **Jyoti** *thinks. She takes
the tie.*

Rasik   Thank you.

Slowly, she starts to loosen his tie. It's sweet, tender.

Jyoti   You did pretty good, Rasik. For a man with a borrowed suit.

Rasik   You think?

Jyoti   Uhuh. And when you *do* go, you'll . . . you'll be like Yudhishthira.

*A second as **Rasik** deciphers that.*

Rasik   . . . Like the Pandavas Yudhishthira?

Jyoti   You're going to climb a mountain to heaven, with Steve instead of a dog for company, you're going find your brothers, your sisters. And you're going to tell them who you were. That you lived for them.

Rasik   You believe that?

Jyoti   I do, if you do.

Rasik   Classic story, beautiful story.

He looks into her eyes, they hold the look. They haven't done this in years.

She starts to unbutton his shirt. He flinches as she gets a few buttons down, suddenly self-conscious.

Jyoti   It's ok. No one's here.

Rasik   Heh.

He nods, she continues. She removes his shirt, leaving him in his vest. He looks frail, vulnerable. But ready. He looks at her.

Jyoti   Ready?

He gives her a thumbs up. Slowly, she wheels him towards the water.

You better not die.

Rasik   I won't.

Jyoti *starts to wheel him in.*

Jyoti   Because I swear, if you make even this moment all about you . . .

Rasik *moves off into the water.* **Jyoti** *watches him go. He turns to her.*

Rasik   What do you see?

Jyoti   I see . . .

A beat.

Wide angle.

Rasik *continues to move away.*

A beautiful night on the Dandi coast. The sand still soft from an afternoon shower, the stars bright and freshly washed, the swish-sway of the waves and standing on the shore, our intrepid heroine!

That's me. And she looks fucking great.

Better now than ever, and as she stands there, looking fucking great, she brings her eyes to the horizon and there . . .

She flies through the images.

Mother sings as she hangs a sheet.

Three suitors walk home empty handed, kicking cans down the street.

Father cries through a bottle in his hands.

Kirit Kumar shouts goodbye from a sinking ship.

My grandsons wave sparklers in the garden.

My sister carves our names into a tree.

My sisters raise their fists into the sky.

My daughter's lonely in an office but she'd never want to say.

My daughter's hungover on a sofa, laughing at her day.

David . . . closes early to learn Johnny Cash and as our heroine steps towards the sea we expect a close up, she deserves the close up, and it doesn't come. But why?

Because she wasn't brave? No.

Because she wasn't fierce? No.

Because she needed love? Heh. No.

Because she needed someone to shout at? That's a nice line, that'll do.

And there in the water, she spots, yes, crash zoom as she spots him, she spots a shape to shout at, a shape she's known her whole life and –

RASIK! RASIK!

And she knows, she knows their Great Adventure was a lie, she probably knew it from the start but –

You're far out, Rasik! You're too far out

You're too far

You're too

He disappears.

You're

Rasik.

She waits.

Hey!

She waits.

She waits.

She waits.

Then **Rasik** *rises. Renewed, replenished. Sitting in 'Steve' like it's a throne.*

His younger self rises alongside him, hers skips in from the shadows.

And **Rasik** *and* **Jyoti** *look at each other across the distance, like that first time a lifetime ago.*

Her, curious. Him, dripping. They call out . . .

Rasik   It was never meant to be a lie!

Jyoti   I know!

Rasik   That said.

We never did go to Blackpool.

Jyoti   I don't want to go to Blackpool, Rasik.

Rasik   So where'd you want to go?

Jyoti *thinks. Steps towards him.*

Jyoti   Oh you old bastard.

She sighs.

Let's go home.

End